Life in
God's Garden

Life in
God's Garden

Steven J. Campbell
with
Austin J. Campbell

Books for the Harvest
Farmington, New Mexico

Life in God's Garden

© 2015 by Steven J. Campbell
Austin J. Campbell

Authors grant permission for any non-commercial reproduction to promote the Kingdom of God.

All other rights reserved.

Published by:

Books for the Harvest
Farmington, New Mexico
USA

ISBN-13: 978-0692546512

ISBN-10: 0692546510

Cover design by Austin J. Campbell

Chapter 7—The Enclosed Garden by Austin J. Campbell

Acknowledgments

As with all authors, I am the product of the influence of many others. Even so, I have been primarily influenced by the Word of God. As I have read and meditated on it, the Bible has shaped my life more than anything else has. Through my personal study, as well as through reading and hearing what others have said, the Holy Spirit has made the Word of God come alive in my life. Therefore, I first acknowledge the Holy Spirit as having the greatest influence in my life—leading me to the love of the Father and to salvation through Jesus Christ.

Also, I want to acknowledge my family, friends, colleagues, other authors, ministers, and churches. All of these have shaped me as a person and as an author. Even though I am not able to acknowledge each one individually, I do want to thank a few people who made this book possible:

> Susan, my wife—who encouraged me to write even when I thought I could not. Her influence in my life is beyond measure.

> Our eight children—each one of you helped me to understand the love of the Heavenly Father better. I want to give a special thanks to Austin, my son, for writing a chapter in this book and for designing the cover, and to my daughter Angela for her amazing picture on the front cover of this book, and to my

daughter Anna for taking the photograph on the back cover of this book.

My pastor, Christie DeWees—I thank you for writing the foreword to this book and for all your help and encouragement throughout the years.

My church, World Harvest Center in Farmington, New Mexico—for accepting my family and me and allowing us to grow in Christ with each of you.

Finally, I thank all the unnamed family, friends, colleagues, authors, ministers, and churches for their influence in my life.

Contents

Foreword

Life in God's Garden will change your perspective about God and you will discover rich insight that has been often hidden in the pages of the familiar passages of the Word of God. This powerful book gives you an in-depth look into biblical secrets that will open your eyes and your heart to what God has for you.

Regardless of your current walk with the Lord Jesus Christ and where you find yourself on the road; this book will encourage and build your faith and love toward God.

Steven Campbell and Austin Campbell dig deep into the Scripture to bring you to a greater awareness of our availability to function and live in all that God has for us.

Through God's eyes you will discover:

- What is it like to live in the Garden now?
- Insight to the ground, the fruit and how it is related to you.
- Secrets to finding what you have longed for in relationship with God.

Once and for all we can take revelation concerning the profound truths in this book and walk in His love and purpose owning the victory that is ours.

"A locked up garden is my sister, my bride;
A locked up spring,
A sealed fountain."
(Song of Solomon 4:12 WEB)

—*Christie DeWees*
Senior Pastor
World Harvest Center
Farmington, New Mexico
USA

Introduction

I invite you to use your God-given imagination as I attempt to portray what life in the Garden of Eden was like. As you do this, the Holy Spirit can make this past event come alive and apply its lessons to your life, for there are lessons for each one of us to learn from humanity's first days on earth.

No doubt, as you use your imagination the Holy Spirit will show you things from the Scriptures that I never thought of, just as you will read things in this book that you have never thought of. Plus, as you join your thoughts with the thoughts contained in this book, God's brilliance in creating a Garden for humanity to live in will be magnified. The fact is that we all only see a part of the picture, but as we put our pieces together, the magnificence of God's creation increases.

Looking back, Adam and Eve had an amazing adventure with God in the Garden of Eden. Unfortunately, this amazing life in the Garden came to an abrupt end. Yet, God did not give up on humanity even though He had to remove them from the Garden.

Throughout the pages of this book, I will continually reference what life was like for the first couple in the Garden of Eden. By doing this, you will learn more about your own relationship with God. Briefly, this is what this book is about—your relationship to God and your relationship to others. Additionally, you will understand how God is continuing to meet with you in a garden this very day. And within His garden, you will discover how unique and special you are to God since He can live within and through you like no other person. You are His special creation!

You were created to live in a garden-type environment, which will be your eternal home—paradise.[1] Even so, there is a garden-type life that God wants you to experience now—*Life in God's Garden.*

---

[1] see Luke 23:43 and Revelation 2:7.

Chapter 1

What Is a Garden?

I t is spoken of throughout the world, but its importance rarely understood. Yet, it was one of the most important parts of God's original creation. Even so, it seems to have vanished. However, through the pages of this book it is my hope that you will know this creation still exists today.

What is the original creation that still exists? It's God's garden. Instantly, this may raise questions such as these in your mind: Are you saying that the Garden of Eden still exists? How can this be? Where would it be? If it exists, is it possible to live there now?

Most believe, as I did, that God's garden totally vanished millenniums ago; nevertheless, I want to show you in what way it still exists. But before I do that, I want to explore with you what a garden is like.

God created all things.[1] One of the least understood of His creation is a garden. The Bible tells us that:

> The Lord God planted a garden eastward in
> Eden . . . (Genesis 2:8)

What is a garden? A garden is the invention of God. It is something He thought of; it came from His heart.

---

[1] see John 1:3.

He made the first garden that became a blueprint for all gardens to come. Now, stay with me as we quickly look at two technical definitions. Then after that, we will make some simple observations.

First, let's look at the definition of a garden from the dictionary:

> 1. A piece of ground appropriated to the cultivation of herbs, fruits, flowers, or vegetables.
> 2. A rich, well-cultivated spot or tract of country.[2]

Second, let's look at the word for *garden* in the original Hebrew language of the Bible:

> gan—as a noun, masculine/feminine:
> a garden, an enclosure.[3]

Now, I want to give you my definition of a garden while applying these definitions with the fact that gardens originated in the heart of God. My simple definition of a garden is: *a well-defined area made for the pleasure and/or fulfillment of the one designing it and for the one(s) who will enjoy it.*

Since this is a book based on the Bible, let's check this definition with the Scriptures. First, we notice:

> *God looked over everything he had made; it was so good, so very good! (Genesis 1:31 TMSG)*

---

[2] Webster's Revised Unabridged Dictionary of the English Language.

[3] Brown-Driver-Briggs Hebrew Lexicon—Abridged.

We see from this verse that God was very pleased with everything He made, which included the Garden of Eden. God made everything for His pleasure—especially His garden in Eden. He so enjoyed His garden that He loved to walk in it in the cool of the day.[4]

The Garden of Eden was a special area within a part of the earth called Eden. It seemed to have been an enclosed area; since after Adam and Eve sinned, the way to the Garden was blocked by God so they could not get to the tree of life.[5]

We also see that what God planted in the Garden was for the pleasure and fulfillment of mankind—a pleasure to look at and good for food (fulfillment):

> *The Lord God planted a garden eastward in Eden, and there He put the man whom He had formed. And out of the ground the Lord God made every tree grow that is pleasant to the sight and good for food. (Genesis 2:8–9)*

The Garden was God's invention designed for His pleasure and fulfillment and for the pleasure and fulfillment of mankind—mankind needed what was in the Garden of Eden. Since that time, the Garden has been replicated on a limited basis throughout the earth. In other words, since mankind carries the image of God within them, they want to make gardens. At this time, I want to give my definition of a garden again, and then encourage you to look at some famous gardens that mankind has made.

---

[4] see Genesis 3:8.
[5] see Genesis 3:24.

A garden is: *a well-defined area made for the* **pleasure** and/or **fulfillment** *of the one designing it and for the one(s) who will enjoy it.*

Famous Gardens

No doubt, the Garden of Eden is the most famous garden ever. In the next chapter, we will look at this famous garden God made in some detail. However, before we do that I want to encourage you to look at other famous gardens in the world, which may help you to understand the makeup of a garden.

Every country has beautiful gardens to enjoy. Since we live in the age of the Internet, you can easily view these famous gardens on your electronic device by simply searching for the famous gardens in your country, or in the whole world. I know you will be amazed, as I was, at the different gardens that mankind has made. Some have striking colors and others have intricate designs. Some are quite simple while others are more elaborate. Each garden is designed for the fulfillment of the one who designed it and for those who will experience its uniqueness.

As you view these many famous gardens, it will be obvious that God really started something in making that first garden in Eden. Mankind needed and enjoyed that first garden and ever since that time there has been a desire in their heart to reproduce that garden-type experience. Even some of the largest cities have famous garden-type areas—New York City has Central Park, Chicago has Lincoln Park, and the list could go on. Since mankind's first home was in a garden, it seems apparent that we have never lost that desire to be close to a garden-type environment.

My definition for a garden emphasized the words *"pleasure* and *fulfillment"* since this is the major purpose of a garden. However, we could have included several others words in our definition, such as: satisfaction, enjoyment, happiness, delight, etc.

Humans were made to experience a garden-type atmosphere. Actually, I believe we were made to *live* in a garden-type reality. This book will explore this idea and hopefully help increase your desire to experience *Life in God's Garden* in its fullness. I believe He created us for this.

In the next chapter we explore what life was like in God's garden—the Garden of Eden.

Chapter 2

The First Garden

mazing! Awesome! Fantastic! Breathtaking! Nothing else like it! No doubt, these words and many others could be used to describe the place God created for man to live in. How wonderful would it be if the Garden of Eden still existed today? If it did still exist, what would it be like now?

Before we answer these questions, we will first look to see what the Garden of Eden was like and then what its purpose was. We will reference several Scriptures in doing this. Let's begin with these verses:

> *God looked over everything he had made; it was so good, so very good! . . . Heaven and Earth were finished, down to the last detail. (Genesis 1:31–2:1 TMSG)*

God created everything in heaven and earth and it was exceedingly good. Included in His creation of the earth was a very special place, a garden. We know it was very special since He placed in it the greatest of His creation—mankind.

> *The Lord God planted a garden eastward in Eden, and there He put the man whom He had formed. (Genesis 2:8)*

What Was Life Like in the Garden?

The first thing to observe in the verse just quoted is that *"the **Lord God** planted a garden."* This garden was a special creation by God Himself! He alone has limitless capabilities in creating a garden. If you took my advice in the last chapter and used the Internet to look at the famous gardens in the world, then I expect you were amazed at the seemingly limitless possibilities in gardening. But keep in mind that these were merely human creations. Even so, each person does carry a measure of God's creativity; however, God embodies *all* creativity. If humans have made such astounding gardens, what kind of a garden did God make?

Although we do not know exactly what the Garden of Eden was like, we know that after God created it, **He said** that it was very good.[1] When God says something is very good, then it is immeasurably good.

Since human beings carry God's creativity, perhaps the Garden of Eden included some of the best features of the famous gardens of the world. Nevertheless, we do not have to speculate on all the aspects of the Garden because the Scriptures give us several details about it. These details are what we will examine now. One of the first of these is found in Genesis 2:9:

> *And out of the ground the Lord God made every tree grow that is pleasant to the sight and good for food. . . .*

---

[1] see Genesis 1:31.

The first plants listed in the Garden were trees, which is a very significant point. In fact, in writing this chapter I now view trees in a different light. I notice more of God's creativity in His vast variety of trees—how each one has a purpose. From my definition of a garden, a tree's purpose is for God's pleasure and for the pleasure and fulfillment of the one(s) who will enjoy it.

The first trees listed in the previous verse are *"every tree . . . that is pleasant to the sight."* These would be trees that are ornamental—those desirable for their appearance—pleasing to the eyes.

We now come to a challenging part for you as the reader. Yet, if you stay with me as I list some trees that were probably in the Garden, and if you will read slowly, thinking about what each one looks like, it will help make a very important point—God is a **good** God.

Ornamental Trees:

> Red Bud, Dogwood, Magnolia, Wisteria, Tulip, Acacia, Cypress, Sycamore, Aspen, Holly, Lebanon Cedar, Weeping Willow, Oak, Norway Spruce, Blue Spruce, Pine, Yew, Birch, Maple, Beech, Myrtle, Broom, Terebinth, and Palm Trees to name a few. *(Note: you may need to look on the Internet at some of the above trees to see their beauty.)*

The next trees that are listed in the aforementioned verse are *"every tree . . . that is . . . good for food."* This would include fruit trees and nut trees. Please read as I suggested above (slowly, thinking about each tree). By doing this, you will see more of the care of God toward humanity.

Fruit and Nut Trees:

> Apple, Peach, Cherry, Plum, Apricot, Pear, Orange, Grapefruit, Lime, Lemon, Banana, Pomegranate, Mango, Mulberry, Persimmon, Olive, Fig, Coconut, Date Palm, Avocado, Walnut, Almond, Pecan, Filbert, Ginkgo, Chestnut, Butternut, Hazelnut, Cashew and others.

Why did I list all of these trees? It is to help us to think about all of the trees in the Garden—so many varieties were there. In fact, the Bible says, *"And out of the ground the Lord God made **every** tree grow that is pleasant to the sight and good for food"* (*emphasis added*).[2] From this verse it appears (especially in the original Hebrew) that God made every one of the trees that were ornamental and every one of the trees that were good for food grow in the Garden. At the very least, we can say that there was an enormous variety of trees in the Garden of Eden. Why is this fact so important? For two reasons:

First, it shows how **good** God is. God provided for humanity with this multitude of trees. Actually, for their enjoyment, He gave them every kind of tree that there was. And out of this huge multitude of trees, only one warning was given about one tree! This warning was for the good of mankind. The truth is, God has *always* been very good to humanity.

---

[2] see Genesis 2:9.

A second reason this enormous variety of trees is significant is shown in the rest of the verse:

> *. . . The tree of life was also in the midst of the garden, and the tree of the knowledge of good and evil. (Genesis 2:9)*

Out of all of the wonderful trees that God planted in the Garden, two were individually mentioned. Why? Because they were very special. How were they special? Unlike the other trees that met mankind's physical needs—*"pleasant to the sight and good for food"*—these two trees dealt with deeper issues than the physical nature. These two trees sorted out the deep issues of life!

These issues will be covered in greater depth in the coming chapters, but for now, we want to stay on the point of what life was like in the Garden.

The Garden was full of beautiful and fruitful trees, with the very center of the Garden occupied with two unique trees. I believe these two trees were not hidden in the midst of other trees but stood out side-by-side in the middle of God's garden. I believe this is why God never said that they could not *look at* the tree of the knowledge of good and evil—because you could not help but see it. God only said they could not eat from it.

Staying on point of what life in the Garden was like; we see there were grasses, herbs, trees, animals, creeping things, birds, and of course, mankind.[3] To summarize what the Garden of Eden was like, it was FULL of life.

---

[3] see Genesis chapters one and two.

Additionally, we notice that the Garden was watered by a mist from the earth and by a river.[4] So it appears that God took care of the watering, but man was responsible for cultivating the Garden.

> *The LORD God took the man and put him in the Garden of Eden to work it and take care of it. (Genesis 2:15 NIV)*

Man had a lot to take care of, but it was easy work— no toil or sweat. A large part of man's work was to name *all* of the birds and animals as God brought them to him.

> *Out of the ground the Lord God formed every beast of the field and every bird of the air, and brought them to Adam to see what he would call them. And whatever Adam called each living creature, that was its name. So Adam gave names to all cattle, to the birds of the air, and to every beast of the field. . . . (Genesis 2:19–20)*

There was plenty of activity in the Garden. There were creatures in the air and creatures on the ground, all needing to be named. I believe a part of man taking dominion over the creatures of the air and land was when he named them. Could it be that by Adam naming the creatures, it brought forth their character, their personality? Of course, this character and personality was before sin entered the world. Since sin entered the world, their characteristics have been perverted. Even

---

4 see Genesis 2:6 and 2:10.

so, their original character and personality that was in the Garden of Eden will be restored when Jesus returns and restores all things:

> *The wolf will romp with the lamb, the leopard sleep with the kid. Calf and lion will eat from the same trough, and a little child will tend them.*
>
> *Cow and bear will graze the same pasture, their calves and cubs grow up together, and the lion eat straw like the ox.*
>
> *The nursing child will crawl over rattlesnake dens, the toddler stick his hand down the hole of a serpent.*
>
> *Neither animal nor human will hurt or kill on my holy mountain. . . . (Isaiah 11:6–9 TMSG)*

I believe that mankind will play an important part in this restoration process since God said we are to have dominion (rule over) His creatures.[5]

Life was wonderful in the Garden. However, even with all the life, all the activity, and God Himself in the Garden, there was a major problem! Really? How could that be? Because even as Adam was busy with all of God's creation in the Garden, he was still alone. What? Alone? God was there. Every bird and animal was there. How was he alone? He had no human fellowship. But was human fellowship necessary when Adam already had fellowship with God and with all of creation?

[5] see Genesis 1:26–28.

The answer lies in the heart of God. Remember, humans were created in God's image. What does that mean? It means God initiated human fellowship. To say it another way, something in the heart of God wanted human fellowship for Himself. He was not satisfied with all He created until He created humans—men and women. This need for human fellowship was birthed in God's heart first; then, since we are created in His image, we also need human fellowship—even when we have God living among us, or even in us.

What was life in the Garden like? For the most part, it was a constant flow of new experiences. Besides experiencing the things of the Garden itself, there seemed to be endless new experiences as God brought creatures to Adam daily to name. These new experiences with each new creature were so exhilarating for Adam and God—who thoroughly enjoyed watching His man interact with each new creature.

But something else was happening at the same time and it was not good. For with each new creature brought before Adam, the incompleteness of man became more evident. It seemed that each day God and man felt the incompleteness afresh. Finally, when the last of the creatures did not fulfill man's need, God did.

He put the man in a deep sleep before creating the woman to show that man cannot meet his own deep-seated needs; it takes the power of God working on his behalf. This is a lesson for all of us—only through God can all of our deep-seated needs be met.

Here is something else for us to consider. We do not know how long it took Adam to name *all* of the animals that God brought to him. For sure it took time, a minimum of several weeks or even months. Why does this matter? Because that is the length of time before the woman was created.

This brings another question to mind, "What if that amount of time was necessary for Adam's aloneness to be *fully* felt?" I am not just talking about Adam feeling alone, for it appears from the Scriptures that Adam may not have realized how alone he was, though he surely felt something was missing in his life. It was **God** who pointed out that Adam was alone! He is the One who felt Adam's aloneness.

Is it possible that the woman was not created until *God* fully felt Adam's aloneness? For God felt what Adam felt, only deeper.[6] In other words, God's heart needed a bride just as Adam's did. Remember, in heaven Jesus already had all of the living creatures, the seraphim, the cherubim, the angels, and numerous things we do not even know about and He still wanted/needed a bride. Because of this, He will present to Himself a beautiful, pure bride just as He did for Adam. Ephesians 5:27–32 speaks of this and Adam's response to the Lord when He created woman:[7]

> *that He might present her to Himself a glorious church, not having spot or wrinkle or any such thing, but that she should be holy and without blemish. . . . For we are members of His body, of His flesh and of His*

---

[6] see Psalm 139.
[7] see Genesis 2:23.

bones. "For this reason a man shall leave his father and mother and be joined to his wife, and the two shall become one flesh." This is a great mystery, but I speak concerning Christ and the church.

In summary, "What was life in the Garden of Eden like?" Amazingly Wonderful! Breathtaking! Why? God walked there. He worked "hand-in-hand" with Adam by personally bringing all the animals He created to Adam to name. He watched over all of His creation, especially mankind. When He saw Adam was alone, He created the perfect helper, the perfect companion for him. This very scenario would be repeated about 4000 years later when Jesus walked among humanity. That is to say, the Father would not leave His new creation[8] alone when Jesus left, but gave us the perfect helper, the perfect companion—the Holy Spirit.

Now we will look at the God's purpose for making the Garden of Eden.

The Garden's Purpose

The definition I gave for a garden emphasizes the point that the Garden of Eden was made for God and for man. In this chapter, I will concentrate on the Garden being made for mankind. In the coming chapters, I will emphasize how it was made for God.

The purpose of the Garden of Eden was to fulfill *all of mankind's needs.* In looking at some of those needs, we will see some specific purposes of the Garden.

---

[8] see 2 Corinthians 5:17.

First, we see in Genesis 2:15 that mankind needed responsibilities—something to do.

> *God took the Man and set him down in the Garden of Eden to work the ground and keep it in order.* (TMSG)

One of the major purposes of the Garden was for humanity to learn to rest in the work of the Lord—to do only what He gave them to do. In the above verse, we notice that they were originally *only* responsible for the Garden of Eden and not the rest of the earth, for the only work God told them to do was in the Garden. He did not tell them to do any work outside of the Garden.

We need things to do but only what He gives us to do. This is the very example Jesus set for us to follow— He only did what the Father gave Him to do.[9]

The Tree of Life Version does an excellent job of translating the Hebrew words in Genesis 2:15 as:

> *Then ADONAI Elohim took the man and gave him **rest** in the Garden of Eden in order to cultivate and watch over it.* (TLV emphasis added)

A major purpose of God for His people has always been to enter into His rest.[10] Mankind failed to do this in the Garden and Israel failed to enter His rest in the wilderness. Even so, One did not fail, the Lord Jesus Christ. Let's follow His example. Let's enter His garden of rest by only doing what He gives us to do.

---

9 see John 6:38.
10 see Hebrews chapters three and four.

A second need of mankind was to learn to manage free will. This was another major purpose of God in the Garden of Eden.

> *And the Lord God commanded the man, saying, "Of every tree of the garden you may freely eat; but of the tree of the knowledge of good and evil you shall not eat, for in the day that you eat of it you shall surely die."* *(Genesis 2:16–17)*

There could not be free will if God did not give mankind a choice. These verses set the choice before them—obey or disobey—their choice. They failed. In fact, since that time ALL have failed to a greater or lesser degree except One. We are to follow the example of the last Adam (Jesus) not the first Adam. Jesus always chose to obey.[11] By His grace we can also choose to obey.[12]

A third need of mankind was to learn to interact with all of nature—especially the animal kingdom, which was another major purpose of life in the Garden.

> *So the Lord God formed from the ground all the wild animals and all the birds of the sky. He brought them to the man to see what he would call them, and the man chose a name for each one. He gave names to all the livestock, all the birds of the sky, and all the wild animals. . . . (Genesis 2:19–20 NLT)*

---

[11] see Hebrews 4:14–15.
[12] see Hebrews 4:16.

Adam did not just quickly name the animals. He first interacted with them in their environment and then He named them based upon his interaction with them. I believe, as others do also, that Adam and Eve could communicate back and forth with the animals (including the birds). I believe that through this communication Adam was able to name the animals more accurately. You may or may not believe as I do, but for sure there was at least one animal that they could communicate with—the serpent. In fact, they did not even seem surprised that the serpent could communicate so easily with them.[13] Also, you may remember that God opened the mouth of a donkey and it communicated with Balaam quite remarkably, even about their past history together.[14]

I believe that if God could open the mouth of an animal, He could just as easily close the mouth of an animal. This seems to be what He did sometime after the fall of man into sin since serpents or no other animals talk to us now.

Humanity's interaction with nature was interrupted because of sin. Therefore, humanity is still learning to interact with all of nature—the earth, the environment, and the animals.

A fourth purpose of the Garden was mankind's need to learn intimacy with God and with others. This is still the major purpose in all of life—to learn to love.

Jesus said to him, "'You shall love the Lord your God with all your heart, with all your

---

[13] see Genesis 3:1–5.
[14] see Numbers 22:28–30 and 2 Peter 2:16.

> *soul, and with all your mind.' This is the first*
> *and great commandment. And the second is*
> *like it: 'You shall love your neighbor as*
> *yourself.'" (Matthew 22:37–39)*

Without other human beings, mankind would not have learned to love as God intended. Remember, we cannot really love God unless we love others.[15] That is why when Adam just loved God and His creation, it was not enough; he needed other human beings to love.

> *God said, "It's not good for the Man to be*
> *alone; I'll make him a helper, a companion."*
> *... God put the Man into a deep sleep. As he*
> *slept he removed one of his ribs and replaced*
> *it with flesh. God then used the rib that he*
> *had taken from the Man to make Woman*
> *and presented her to the Man. (Genesis*
> *2:18–22 TMSG)*

God knew that mankind would never learn to love as they should without other human beings, therefore God made them male and female so that they could marry and have a family—which is where love is to be learned first.[16]

A fifth need of mankind in the Garden was to learn to interact with the devil properly—to use the word of God as a sword.[17]

> *Now the serpent was more cunning than any*
> *beast of the field which the Lord God had*

---

[15] see 1 John 4:20.

[16] see 1 Timothy 5:8.

[17] see Ephesians 6:17.

made. And he said to the woman, "Has God indeed said, 'You shall not eat of every tree of the garden'?" (Genesis 3:1)

When Jesus was tempted by the devil, He relied on the Word of God.[18] However, when Eve was being tempted by the serpent, Adam did not run to her defense with the word of God. Instead, he just stood there silently[19] not using his greatest weapon against the devil—the sword of the Spirit, which is the word of God.

(NOTE: When I write "the word of God" I'm referring to *all* the ways God speaks to us (the voice of the Spirit, dreams, visions, through others, etc. But when I capitalize *word* as "the Word of God," I'm referring to the Bible.)

Like a lion, the devil seeks to devour us, but we need to have more faith in God to keep us from his deceptions than faith in the devil to deceive us. Without a doubt, learning to use the word of God against the devil is a very important lesson to learn.[20]

In summary, the purpose of the Garden of Eden was to perpetuate all the life that God had created, which includes mankind. And if mankind would have taken his dominion in the Garden, the maximum life would have come forth, instead, they submitted to the devil and death came forth.

The following is a question to consider. Was the initial plan of God to have all of mankind dwell in the Garden of Eden? It appears not to be so since God's

---

[18] see Matthew 4:1–11.
[19] see Genesis 3:6.
[20] see pages 47–48 for more on this subject.

original blessing upon mankind was to multiply and *fill* the earth:

> *God blessed them and said to them, "Be*
> *fruitful and increase in number; fill the earth*
> *and subdue it. . . ." (Genesis 1:28 NIV)*

Humans were to cover the whole earth, not just the Garden. There is something more to consider here. Could it be that it was God's original plan for each family to establish their own garden-type environment as they filled the whole earth? If so, there would have been multiplied unique gardens expanding across the globe. Each household would have had their own "garden" since Genesis 2:24 shows us that we are to leave our initial family and establish our own household:

> *For this cause will a man go away from his*
> *father and his mother and be joined to his*
> *wife; and they will be one flesh. (Genesis*
> *2:24 BBE)*

I think that when Jesus returns to earth He will restore all things to a Garden-of-Eden-type-condition. Therefore, it could be assumed that the earth was to be filled with a garden-type environment as the people went out from the original garden. In other words, perhaps the Garden of Eden was to be replicated throughout the earth as families increased in number.

It does appear that God did not want humanity living all in one place. Actually, He wanted them scattered throughout the whole earth.[21]

---

[21] see Genesis 1:28.

We see this as people began to say:

> *Then they said, "Come, let's build a great city*
> *for ourselves with a tower that reaches into*
> *the sky. This will make us famous and keep*
> *us from being scattered all over the world."*
> *(Genesis 11:4 NLT)*

But when the Lord saw what they were trying to do,
He scattered them throughout the earth:

> *. . . the Lord scattered them all over the*
> *world, and they stopped building the city.*
> *(Genesis 11:8 NLT)*

The possibility of God wanting a garden-type
environment filling the whole earth deserves
consideration. Even so, I am not dogmatic about it.
However, it does appear to be the case, or at least close
to it, in the millennium—the time of the restoration of
all things. This is the time when Jesus returns to the
earth as King.[22]

In the next chapter, we will reveal the garden of God
that exists today.

---

[22] see Acts 3:20–21.

Chapter 3

The Garden Today

O ne of the things the devil wants to keep "hush-hush" is the truth of the garden today. The first two chapters of this book were the beginning of the account of a garden and were necessary for us to realize the truth of the garden today. So let us begin the rest of the story.

The first thing I want to do in this chapter is to answer the questions we asked previously. In the preceding chapters, we asked:

> *Questions from Chapter 1—Are you saying that the Garden of Eden still exists?*
> *How can this be?*
> *Where would it be?*
> *If it exists, is it possible to live there now?*

Here are my answers: Yes, the Garden of Eden still exists. How can that be? Because God had more than one garden in Eden. Actually, He had two gardens in Eden. One still exists today. Where would it be? It is in the entire earth. And yes, it is possible to live there now.

> *Questions from Chapter 2—How wonderful would it be if the Garden still existed today?*
> *If it did still exist, what would it be like now?*

My answers: For sure, it is most wonderful that God's garden still exists today. So what is God's garden like today? It is His delight and joy. It is the most stunning place on earth.

Now, let's look at His garden today and see if you have the same reaction to His garden that He has when He looks at it.

Ready?

Then go—go to the closest mirror you have and look into it. You are now looking at the garden of God! Do you see the stunning beauty of His garden? He wants you to.

When God looks at YOU, He sees stunning beauty, brilliant loveliness—it melts His heart. You don't have to take my word for it since we have His reaction in *His own words*. They are found throughout the Song of Solomon. Here are a few of His reactions when He looks at you:

> *Oh, my dear friend! You're so beautiful! (TMSG)*[1]

> *You are beautiful, my darling,*
> *beautiful beyond words. (NLT)*[2]

> *You are altogether beautiful, my darling,*
> *beautiful in every way. (NLT)*[3]

---

[1] see Song of Solomon 1:15.

[2] see Song of Solomon 4:1.

[3] see Song of Solomon 4:7.

You have captured my heart,
my treasure, my bride.
You hold it hostage with one glance of your
eyes . . . (NLT)[4]

How beautiful and how pleasing you are,
O love, with your delights! (TLV)[5]

You are my private garden, *my*
treasure, my bride, (NLT emphasis added)[6]

Do you see what God sees when you look into the mirror? Do you see His stunningly beautiful garden? Of course, we do not see ourselves as beautiful as God does. Why not? Because we have all partaken of the tree of the knowledge of good and evil. Nevertheless, it is time for us to refuse its fruit and only eat from the tree of life (more will be said about this in a later chapter).[7]

We have the same choice as in the original garden— to partake of the tree of life (His words about us) or to partake of the tree of the knowledge of good and evil (our knowledge of what's good and evil about us).

It is time for us to believe God and His view of us more than how we view ourselves. I mean, "Who is correct?" "Is God right?" "Are we right?" Remember, the issue in the Garden with the tree of the knowledge of good and evil was believing what God said about the tree or believing what the devil said about the tree. Adam

---

[4] see Song of Solomon 4:9.

[5] see Song of Solomon 7:7 TLV (in some other versions—7:6).

[6] see Song of Solomon 4:12.

[7] see Chapter 5 of this book.

and Eve believed that partaking of the tree would make them wise and like God. Instead, it only produced death and hiding from God because of how they saw themselves—naked.

It is so important that you believe God's words about you. This is a daily decision, a daily growth. If you want to grow daily, partake of the tree of life—His words.

Wisdom is to keep in mind that we are not changed by looking at the good and evil in our lives, but by looking at Jesus and His glory.

> *But we all, with unveiled face, beholding as in a mirror the glory of the Lord, are being transformed into the same image from glory to glory, just as by the Spirit of the Lord. (2 Corinthians 3:18)*

Jesus is our tree of life. Partake of Him and be His glorious garden.

The Purpose of Today's Garden

God had a purpose for the Garden of Eden beyond my definition of a garden. My definition of a garden is in a general sense. However, man was placed in the Garden of Eden for more than the pleasure and fulfillment of mankind. The Garden was for that, but also for much more. It was for a major purpose—to train mankind for reigning and ruling with Christ.[8]

Now, I want to use the five purposes of the Garden of Eden from the last chapter and apply them to ourselves.

---

[8] see Luke 22:29–30 and Revelation 2:26, 3:21.

The first purpose that we saw was in Genesis 2:15—that mankind needed responsibilities—something to do:

> *God took the Man and set him down in the*
> *Garden of Eden to work the ground and keep*
> *it in order.* (TMSG)

This is a major purpose of God for our lives (His garden). We must "work the ground" (our heart) and keep our lives in order. Seeing as this is such an important purpose in God's garden today, we will not go into greater detail here, but will devote much of the rest of this book to this subject, especially the next chapter.

A second purpose/responsibility of life in God's garden is for us to learn to manage free will. Free will comes into play whenever there is the choice to obey or disobey God. An amazing fact is that Jesus Himself learned obedience. If He had to learn to obey, then we too need to learn this most important lesson—always obey God!

Jesus never failed to obey; however, we have *all* failed to obey in greater or lesser degrees. But just as Jesus learned obedience through the things He suffered, so we will also travel the same road—we will learn obedience throughout our lives.

> *Though he was God's Son, he learned*
> *trusting-obedience by what he suffered, just*
> *as we do. (Hebrews 5:8 TMSG)*

Jesus is our example of what it means to obey God, and the One we are to obey now. For it was through His obedience that He became the author of eternal salvation to all who *obey Him*.[9] Obeying Jesus is where we truly learn to manage free will. We will have more to say about this in a later chapter.[10]

A third purpose/responsibility of life in God's garden is for us to learn to interact with all of nature—especially the animal kingdom. This alarm has gone off in many people today who are called environmentalists. These ones carry a part of God's heart for humanity because we are the ones given dominion over the earth, which God expects us to do in a wise way. Though some environmentalists have taken things too seriously, humanity still has much to learn from them.

Some believe that a major reason why Jesus will return when He does is to keep human beings from completely destroying the earth. Keep in mind that we were given the earth as a sacred trust to tend it and keep it in order.[11] God does hold humans responsible for the earth and will reward those who are obedient to take care of it. So if God has placed a desire in your heart to take care of, or restore any part of nature, obey.

As pointed out above, the animal kingdom is a special responsibility given to humans. God specifically mentions us taking responsibility for them, for when we take care of His creation, we reflect God's nature. We can clearly see this fact in the following Scripture—that humans were created to reflect His nature by taking care of all the earth, especially the animal kingdom.

---

9 see Hebrews 5:9.

10 see Chapter 5 of this book.

11 see Genesis 2:15.

God spoke: "Let us make human beings in our image, make them reflecting our nature

So they can be responsible for the fish in the sea, the birds in the air, the cattle,

And, yes, Earth itself, and every animal that moves on the face of Earth."

God created human beings; he created them godlike,

Reflecting God's nature. He created them male and female.

God blessed them: "Prosper! Reproduce! Fill Earth! Take charge!

Be responsible for fish in the sea and birds in the air, for every living thing that moves on the face of Earth." (Genesis 1:26–28 TMSG)

If God has especially gifted you in this area, then go for it! For you will find pleasure and fulfillment in reflecting this part of God's nature—taking care of His creation.

A fourth purpose/responsibility of life in God's garden is our need to learn intimacy with God and with others, which is the major purpose for all of our lives—to learn to love.

Earlier in this chapter, I stressed the importance that God places on obedience.[12] When Jesus was asked about the most important thing to obey; He said we are to love God and others.[13]

---

[12] see pages 41–42 of this book.
[13] see Matthew 22:37–39.

Warning! The next few sentences may shock or even offend you, but keep reading and it will all make sense. Here we go: "The greatest commandment has been redefined!" Yes, you read that correctly. The greatest commandment is now redefined—by Jesus' life. Let that sink in for a moment before jumping to the next paragraph.

How can this be true? Because there is a new standard of love and a new power of love. What is that new standard and power of love? It is the love of God. That is, now we have the power of the same love relationship that the Father and Son has. This new standard of love is the love that we are to abide in. Because of the depth of love that the Father has for the Son, this is one of the greatest passages in Scripture:

> *"I've loved you the way my Father has loved me. Make yourselves at home in my love."*
> *(John 15:9 TMSG)*

Another of the greatest passages in Scripture is when Jesus speaks of the Father saying:

> *". . . You have sent Me, and have loved them as You have loved Me." (John 17:23)*

The Father and Son both love us as they love each other! Let your heart take hold of this fact and it will revolutionize your life!—you will enter the garden experience you are meant to abide in. God's love is our "tree of life." In fact, it is our eternal life. Jesus said it well in the following verse:

"And this is eternal life, that they may know You, the only true God, and Jesus Christ whom You have sent." (John 17:3)

Jesus is speaking here of an intimate knowing—a knowing of the very heart of God—His very nature. God is love and He wants us to know that intimately, not just in fact. He wants us to enjoy who He is. He is very emotional and He wants us to experience His emotions—His feelings toward us. He *delights* in us!

God delights in YOU! This may be hard for you to believe so I will let the word of God speak for itself:

> *The Lord directs the steps of the godly.*
> **He delights in every detail** *of their lives.*
> *Though they stumble, they will never fall,*
> *for the Lord holds them by the hand. (Psalm 37:23–24 NLT emphasis added)*

Now, continuing to look at the new standard and power of love, we see that what was considered as the two greatest commandments were based upon mankind's ability to love.[14] But the new commandment is higher; it is based upon what mankind cannot do on his own. As Jesus is getting ready to go back to the Father,[15] He said:

> *So now I am giving you a new commandment: Love each other. Just as I have loved you, you should love each other. (John 13:34 NLT)*

---

[14] see Matthew 22:37–39.
[15] see John 13:1.

Do you see how this is a higher commandment? Here is how it is higher: Now, we are to follow the supreme example of love lived before us—Jesus Christ. We are to love as Jesus did; He loved the Father and others perfectly. This love requires an ability beyond our own; it requires the very Spirit of Christ—the Holy Spirit. As others have said, "It takes God to love God." The Bible says it this way:

> *We have the power of loving, because he first had love for us. (1 John 4:19 BBE)*

We have been given the Holy Spirit; we have His power to love. We do not love God with just our own strength of heart, soul, and mind. To say it another way, we do not just love God with our own strength; we love Him with the added power of Christ—the Holy Spirit.

Remember that the second of the "greatest commandments" spoke of loving others as you love yourself. But now, Jesus commands you to love others just as He did. This is a higher commandment. Again, it requires more than your own strength (which only results in your loving others as yourself); it requires the power of Christ to love others as He did.

When you love as Christ Jesus did, *you will be obeying* the "greatest commandments," and on top of that, His new commandment. The maximum joy (pleasure and fulfillment) in your life as God's garden will be found when you love as Jesus Christ did. This is clearly seen in the following passage of Scripture:

> *"I've loved you the way my Father has loved me. Make yourselves at home in my love. If*

you keep my commands, you'll remain intimately at home in my love. That's what I've done—kept my Father's commands and made myself at home in his love.

"I've told you these things for a purpose: that my joy might be your joy, and your joy wholly mature. This is my command: Love one another the way I loved you. This is the very best way to love. Put your life on the line for your friends." (John 15:9–13 TMSG)

A fifth purpose/responsibility of life in God's garden is for us to learn to interact with the devil properly—to use the word of God as our sword. In the beginning when mankind did not use the word of God against the word of the serpent (the devil), death began. Death began because the word of God was not used against his lies. Since that time, the necessary weapon to defeat the devil's lies is the word of God. God's word is always more powerful than the lies of the devil, so believe God's word and you will walk in the fullness of life.

The devil is the father of lies, there is no truth in him.[16] Jesus is the truth; there is no lie in Him.[17] Jesus used truth to defeat the lies of the devil.[18] He overcame the favorite trick of the devil—misusing the word of God—by rightly using the word of God. Thus, the Bible

[16] see John 8:44.
[17] see John 14:6.
[18] see Matthew 4:1–11.

shows us how we are to use the sword of the Spirit—the word of God:

A final word: Be strong in the Lord and in his mighty power. Put on all of God's armor so that you will be able to stand firm against all strategies of the devil. For we are not fighting against flesh-and-blood enemies, but against evil rulers and authorities of the unseen world, against mighty powers in this dark world, and against evil spirits in the heavenly places.

Therefore, . . . take the sword of the Spirit, which is the word of God. (Ephesians 6:10–17 NLT)

Notice how the word of God is *not* for warring against flesh-and-blood enemies but for warring against evil spirits. Always remember, we are to war *on behalf of* flesh-and-blood enemies by proclaiming the good news—Jesus loves you and will deliver and save you.[19] When you proclaim the word of God you are giving people the opportunity to believe in Him.[20] This is the central purpose of the word of God and the greatest defeat of the devil—the eternal salvation of those who believe in Him. Furthermore, this is one of the greatest joys of life in God's garden—releasing the life you have in Jesus to others.

We will have much more to say about the life in the Word of God (the Bible) in the next chapter.

---

[19] see Matthew 5:43–48.
[20] see Romans 10:13–15.

In summary, the purpose of life in God's garden today (your life) is to enable all of the life that God has created in you to come forth. You are His garden for this reason and for this season. You are to take authority in your garden and release your maximum life potential in all of your relationships. Included in those relationships are God, others, and all of His creation. You are the garden made for God and for mankind—a place for intimate friendship.

A closing thought: Since the spiritual is not first but the natural is[21]—could it be that the Garden of Eden was to be a reflection of what our life should be like? I think so, for we are to be full of life, beauty, fruit, and love for the earth, animals, birds, one another, and God.

---

[21] see 1 Corinthians 15:46.

Chapter 4

The Ground

Soil is a key ingredient for all of life, since God created the plants, the trees, the animals, and the birds out of the ground.[1] Furthermore, He created man from the dust of the ground.[2] Therefore it is safe to say that the ground played a vital role in the creation of life on earth.

I believe God created things from the ground for the same reason that the Garden of Eden, and *all of life,* was not just placed on the earth, but came from the ground—so that it would be a part of the earth. The ground was not the source of life; God was. However, I believe God intended the ground to be a vital part with all of His creation; but when mankind chose to disobey God, the ground was cursed.

> *Then to the man He said, "Because you listened to your wife's voice and ate of the tree which I commanded you, saying, 'You must not eat of it':*
>
> *Cursed is the ground because of you—with pain will you eat of it all the days of your life. . . ." (Genesis 3:17 TLV)*

---

[1] see Genesis 1:12 and 2:19.

[2] see Genesis 2:7.

A careful reading of this verse shows that God did not curse the ground; He simply pronounced the curse that occurred, *"Cursed is the ground because of you."* It was mankind's sin that brought about the ground's curse. Consequently, that which was to be a blessing to all of creation began to bring forth thorns and thistles.[3] Additionally, the ground became mankind's burial place so that he would return to dust.[4]

Even so, the earth is so important to God that Jesus is coming back to restore everything to its proper place *within* the earth.[5] Even the heavenly Father is coming to live on the earth alongside His creation.[6] That is to say; one day all of heaven will be on the new earth. Nevertheless, we do not have to wait for Jesus to return for the restoration to start since all restoration is based upon what He already did on the cross. Specifically, the curse was broken at the cross so all things could be restored. This ongoing process will be completed after Jesus returns to earth.

Jesus, the Master Storyteller

Jesus loved to tell stories; in fact, He was the Master Storyteller. His stories penetrated hearts, changed lives, and are still changing lives to this very day. One reason His stories continue to be so impactful is that He used different parts of creation to tell His stories.

Before we look at some of these, let's see why Jesus loved to use stories in His teachings:

---

[3] see Genesis 3:18.
[4] see Genesis 3:19.
[5] see Acts 3:21.
[6] see Revelation 21:3.

*The disciples came up and asked, "Why do
you tell stories?"*

*He replied, "You've been given insight into
God's kingdom. You know how it works. Not
everybody has this gift, this insight; it hasn't
been given to them. Whenever someone has a
ready heart for this, the insights and
understandings flow freely. But if there is no
readiness, any trace of receptivity soon
disappears. That's why I tell stories: to
create readiness, to nudge the people toward
receptive insight. In their present state they
can stare till doomsday and not see it, listen
till they're blue in the face and not get it."
(Matthew 13:10–13 TMSG)*

Jesus told us stories of natural things to help us
understand spiritual things—things concerning His
kingdom. In this chapter, I will concentrate on two
particular items Jesus used in His stories—the seed and
the ground. Let's begin with this story:

*"Listen! Behold, a sower went out to sow.
And it happened, as he sowed, that some
seed fell by the wayside; and the birds of the
air came and devoured it. Some fell on stony
ground, where it did not have much earth;
and immediately it sprang up because it had
no depth of earth. But when the sun was up it
was scorched, and because it had no root it
withered away. And some seed fell among
thorns; and the thorns grew up and choked*

> *it, and it yielded no crop. But other seed fell on good ground and yielded a crop that sprang up, increased and produced: some thirtyfold, some sixty, and some a hundred."*
> *(Mark 4:3–8)*

There are two things that Jesus highlights in this story—the power of the seed and the power of the soil. He shows us that the seed is very powerful; it has the potential to multiply, even a hundred times. Even so, the multiplying power of the seed may be limited or even eliminated by the condition of the soil. So what do the seed and soil speak of spiritually, and how does it apply to our lives? Thankfully, Jesus explains this story for us so that we can apply it to our lives. He interprets it section by section, as we will do also.

First, we see the seed that fell by the wayside:

> *. . . The seed is the word of God. Those by the wayside are the ones who hear; then the devil comes and takes away the word out of their hearts, lest they should believe and be saved. (Luke 8:11–12)*

We notice from Jesus' explanation that the seed is referring to "the word of God." We also see that "the wayside" ground refers to "their heart." The "seed" had the power to save them but because they did not understand the word,[7] it was snatched from them.

Next, we see the seed that was sown on stony ground:

---

[7] see Matthew 13:19.

But he who received the seed on stony places, this is he who hears the word and immediately receives it with joy; yet he has no root in himself, but endures only for a while. For when tribulation or persecution arises because of the word, immediately he stumbles. (Matthew 13:20–21)

It is important to be deeply rooted and grounded as a follower of Christ given that difficulty and persecution will come because of God's word. Yes, you may initially receive God's word with joy and then be shocked to learn that it will bring suffering and persecution. Therefore, it is a good idea to let new believers know that *"we must go through many hardships to enter the kingdom of God."*[8] Even though we may do this, some will only last for a while before they fall.

Third, we see the seed that fell among the thorns:

Now the ones that fell among thorns are those who, when they have heard, go out and are choked with cares, riches, and pleasures of life, and bring no fruit to maturity. (Luke 8:14–15)

For those who receive God's word this can easily be a major obstacle; as it was in the Garden of Eden. Remember, Eve was tempted by the desire for other things than what God provided.[9] The fruit of that was death.

---

[8] see Acts 14:22.

[9] see Genesis 3:6.

For many, if not most, this is where we find ourselves too often—distracted by the things of this world. Even so, we must keep in mind that most of us will bear the most fruit in whatever life situation we are in. Truly, you may be a dishwasher and bear abundant fruit—the fruit of the Spirit, which is being like Jesus. The issue is to not let the "thorns" crowd out your true life—relationship with Jesus.

The Apostle Paul actually bore the most fruit while in prison. That is, his letters written while imprisoned are still bearing fruit after 2000 years! Considering this, we see that it is not our life situation but our relationship with Jesus that matters. Cherish that relationship by not letting other things crowd it out, which is much easier said than done. Jesus said it this way, *"Seek the Kingdom of God above all else, and live righteously, and he will give you everything you need" (Matthew 6:33 NLT).*

Think about this: God is not too busy or too distracted with the whole universe and all of heaven to spend time with each of us. Therefore, it is hard for us to have a valid excuse of being too busy to spend time with Him since He has the time for us.[10]

The fourth seed fell on good ground:

> *"But he who received seed on the good ground is he who hears the word and understands it, who indeed bears fruit and produces: some a hundredfold, some sixty, some thirty." (Matthew 13:23)*

---

[10] see James 4:8.

We all want to be the one who bears much fruit from what God gives us and the key given here is to hear and understand God's word. To me, to understand this story of the seed and the ground, we need to know that our reactions to the seeds are usually not the "final word" on the subject. What do I mean by that? I mean, just because you failed by being "wayside ground" when you first heard God's word; you may do much better the next time you hear His word. Usually God gives us many chances to increase from "wayside ground" to "good ground." In fact, you may find yourself having all four types of ground at the same time. How? By receiving God's word at different levels—having ground such as these:

"Wayside ground" concerning loving your enemies— but not understanding why you should.

"Stony ground" concerning finances—excited to give to God . . . until the bills come due.

"Thorny ground" concerning spending quality time with God—but being too busy.

"Good ground" concerning compassion—feeling the pain of others and sharing the gospel with them.

We shared all of this from this story (often called the Parable of the Sower) because of the importance of the seed and the ground. You cannot have a garden without first seeding/planting the ground; therefore, the word of God and our heart's receptivity to it needs to be emphasized. We are His garden and He is constantly "seeding" us with His word, which is the source of our life. Jesus said, *Man shall not live by bread alone, but*

by every word that proceeds from the mouth of God"
(Matthew 4:4).

The word of God planted in our hearts produces our growth.[11] And by feeding on the promises in His Word, we become like Christ—partakers of the divine nature.[12] Thus, the Word of God frees us to be Christlike, which is where we find true freedom.

Now, can you imagine what the ground was like in the Garden of Eden? It was perfect. But after mankind sinned, the ground became cursed. So it was with mankind's "ground" (heart); it was perfect before sin, but afterward came under the curse. But now Jesus comes with His word to bless "the ground" and break the curse. Truly, spiritual death can only be broken by the word of God. Even so, though the gospel is preached to all, not all believe His word; but through the goodness of God, the truth is still proclaimed to them.[13]

Speaking about storytelling, I cannot help but wonder if God did not tell stories to Adam and Eve as He walked with them in the Garden of Eden. I believe He did since He loved to tell stories, and He is the same yesterday, today, and forever.[14] I love how the following verses speak of Jesus' storytelling:

> *All Jesus did that day was tell stories—a long storytelling afternoon. His storytelling fulfilled the prophecy:*

---

[11] see 1 Peter 2:2.
[12] see 2 Peter 1:4.
[13] see Romans 10:16–18.
[14] see Hebrews 13:8.

I will open my mouth and tell stories;
I will bring out into the open things
hidden since the world's first day.
(Matthew 13:34–35 TMSG)

What kind of stories did Adam and Eve hear? They were most likely fascinating stories about all of creation and their interaction with each other from God's perspective. The good news is that you are His garden and He will tell you stories as He did Adam and Eve in the "cool of the day"—when all the daily activities are done. This speaks to me of the time when we are least distracted—like when we are asleep. No doubt, our dreams are often God telling us stories to give us better understanding of spiritual things.

Cultivating the Ground

As you remember, humanity's responsibility in the Garden of Eden was to cultivate and watch over it. As God's garden today, we are responsible for cultivating the ground (our heart) and watching over it.[15] How do we cultivate our heart? We cultivate it through love—the love of God and others. The more you love someone, the more you "hang onto every word" spoken—you are listening carefully to them simply because you love them. For sure, this happens easiest when you are first in love.

I am reminded of when I was first in love with my wife. I would make sure I spent time with her, not out of duty or obligation, but out of love. Love compelled me to

---

[15] see Proverbs 4:23.

be with her no matter what I had to do to "free up the time." I was imprisoned by love and never felt freer. Why? I was free to follow my heart; I was not allowing things to crowd out quality time with her. Counting our courtship, we have been seeking each other's presence for over forty-two years. However, like all marriages, we have had our up-and-down times when we let other things crowd out our love. Yet, since love is the greatest compelling force, it has always won out. As the Apostle Paul said, *"Love never fails."*[16]

My wife and I have three girls and we noticed the same power of love with them and their fiancés. They would not allow things to crowd out quality time with each other. Additionally, we have five sons and the same was true of those who became a fiancé—not allowing things to crowd out time with their fiancée.

I am discussing about cultivating the ground, our heart, to receive God's word. The personal examples shared above show how the heart is best cultivated through love. Therefore, love also cultivates our heart to receive the word of God.

An important thing to keep in mind is to rest in God's work. We covered this in an earlier chapter,[17] but I want to emphasize it again. The Tree of Life Version did an excellent job of translating the Hebrew words in Genesis 2:15 as:

> *Then ADONAI Elohim took the man and gave*
> *him **rest** in the Garden of Eden in order to*

---

[16] see 1 Corinthians 13:8.

[17] see page 29.

cultivate and watch over it. (*TLV emphasis added*)

We do not have to strive to love; He has already worked that in us when we were born again. I love how the Bible says it, *"We love, because He first loved us."*[18] I find rest in this fact—I can love because I am loved by Him. I do not have to strive to cultivate my heart; I just have to yield to the love already there. When we realize it is about yielding to His Spirit, then we walk in a new freedom, for His love has set us completely free.[19]

Love is the fuel for a relationship; it catapults you to each other. It springboards you to freedom, for the more love there is, the freer you feel, the freer you are. Consequently, your *ultimate* freedom will be found when you are in heaven. When there, you will be in the presence of the absolute fullness of love, God's love, and His love is extremely personal—you will be loved perfectly and experience perfect freedom! However, you do not have to wait to experience a portion of this because you have the Holy Spirit inside you! You can live in His presence to a large degree now. Even so, the best is yet to come—heaven.[20]

But before we get to heaven, there is something Jesus wants from us—our *first love.* We find this in Revelation chapter two. However, it is interesting to note what Jesus said of the people who had left their first love. He said they were hard workers; they persevered, didn't tolerate evil people, weeded out false

---

[18] see 1 John 4:19.
[19] see 1 John 4:18.
[20] see 1 Corinthians 13:12.

apostles, and patiently suffered for Him without quitting. Even so, Jesus said they needed to repent and do the first works.[21] But does this sound like a people who needed to do more? Could it be that their "first works" were done out of love and the many works since were done out of duty? Probably so, because good works not motivated by the love of God and the love of others, can be easily perverted. The Pharisees are a great example of this.[22]

This brings us to the question, "What is first love?" First love is a constant growing of relationship with a person. It constantly desires to know more about a person for the purpose of relating to them better. For first love is always wanting a greater relationship, it is not satisfied with just staying the same. Therefore, to me, leaving your first love is a prolonged satisfaction with your current level of relationship.

Also, when you keep your first love with Jesus, it is much harder to be unloving to others. Thus, it appears that those Jesus addressed in Revelation chapter two were being unloving toward others—because they had left their first love of Jesus.

It is humbling to admit that I have left my first love of Jesus several times in the forty plus years of being born again. Sad to say, I've had prolonged seasons where I have been satisfied with my knowledge and relationship with the Father, Son, and Holy Spirit. When I have done this, I am much more prone to be unloving to others, even those closest to me. I have been

---

[21] see Revelation 2:5.
[22] see Matthew chapter 23.

the thorny ground Jesus speaks of much too often—allowing other things to choke out my first love.

Recognizing when I am "thorny ground" is the first step of my repentance (change). The next thing I do is forget my failures, or successes, and go back to intimacy.[23] That being said, there are seasons of life when you simply have to speak to your soul. Even King David (a man after God's own heart)[24] had to speak to his soul as shown in Psalm 103. Like David, being in a difficult season of life and having to command yourself out of it, does not mean that you have left your first love. In fact, it seems to show just the opposite when you are refusing to let difficulties dictate the attitude of your heart.

If you desire, pray this prayer with me: "Lord, I am sorry for all the times I have let other things rob me of my first love. I am asking for Your grace to help me to know when I am losing, or have left, my first love. Then give me the grace to help me do what I must do—to repent, to change my path, to turn back to You. I thank You that You will never leave me or forsake me and I want to do the same for You—to always love You first and foremost."

The good news in Jesus' own words is the reward of returning to, and keeping your first love:

> *". . . you have forsaken your first love.*
> *Remember the height from which you have*

---

[23] see Philippians 3:13.
[24] see Acts 13:22.

fallen! Repent and do the things you did at first. . . .

*To him who overcomes, I will give **the right to eat from the tree of life**, which is in the paradise of God."* (Revelation 2:4–7 NIV emphasis added)

The love that God first experienced from humans was in the Garden of Eden. That is, Adam and Eve experienced first love with God. Then they fell from the height of their first love, were forbidden to eat from the tree of life, and experienced death.[25] But if we will return and keep our first love, we will have the right to eat from the tree of life, which is in the paradise of God. This is our "back to the future"—back to the garden-type-realm with the right to eat from the tree of life!

We have been discussing the importance of our first love and now I want to get a little more detailed in the cultivating of our hearts. I said that the heart is best cultivated through love, which is true. Now I want to show you three things that help cultivate love, especially first love. The three things that help cultivate love are the word of God, prayer, and worship.

We have already seen much about the importance of the word of God, which I want to emphasize further. When you are cultivating the ground (your heart), water and seeds are important ingredients. The *word of God* is both the water and the seed.[26] As soon as the seed is planted in good ground and watered, it can grow. Thus,

---

[25] see Genesis 3:22–24.
[26] see Ephesians 5:26.

God's word is the essential ingredient for our freedom to grow. In other words, the word of God never puts you in bondage; it sets you free—free to grow in Christ.

> *Then Jesus said ... "If you abide in My word, you are My disciples indeed. And you shall know the truth, and the truth shall make you free." (John 8:31–32)*

These verses are often misstated as simply, "the truth shall make you free." But freedom is a process that starts with abiding in God's word, which leads to knowing the truth, which leads to freedom. So what is the truth that you will know? It is many faceted, but can be summarized as one thing—God is love! You will know that He **is** love—not just in fact, but also in reality. That is, you will know His love firsthand—He personally loves YOU!

Consequently, without abiding in God's word, you cannot truly be free, since true freedom is to know and to experience God's love. A major cultivator of that love is His Word (the Bible). Sometimes children say it best, as in the song *Jesus Loves Me* that says, "Jesus loves me! This I know, for the Bible tells me so."

You are God's garden and you need the seed and the water of His word. Because of this, the ground, which is your heart, must be cultivated to properly receive His seed and retain His water.

> *This is what the Lord says ...*
> *"Plow up the hard ground of your hearts!*

Do not waste your good seed among thorns."
(Jeremiah 4:3 NLT)

This brings us back to Jesus' story of the seed and the ground that we looked at earlier in this chapter. When Jesus gave this story, along with many others in the Gospel of Matthew, He gave us a major reason for His kingdom stories.

> *He said, "Then you see how every student well-trained in God's kingdom is like the owner of a general store who can put his hands on anything you need, old or new, exactly when you need it." (Matthew 13:52 TMSG)*

A major reason for Jesus' stories is for you to be trained well in His kingdom so that you can help others. It is not just about how you receive the seed since your reception of the seed affects the fruit in your life and in the lives of others. You should be able to share with others what they need when they need it; whether it is old things—things you have learned/experienced before or new things—fresh experiences, fresh revelation from the Lord. By doing this, you are showing your love for God and for others.

You are God's garden and if you have good ground, you will bear much fruit—thirty, sixty, or even a hundred times what was planted in you. This obviously speaks of more than just the fruit in your life; it speaks of your life being multiplied in others.

A second love cultivator is *prayer*. Since prayer is so vital in cultivating our love, many chapters could be written on this subject. However, this would be beyond the purpose of this book. (If you have enjoyed my writings, I have written several chapters on this subject in my book *WELL DONE: Good and Faithful Servant*.) But for this book, I want to point out only a few things as they relate to God's garden.

First, I want to compare prayer to the "cool-of-the-day-time" when God would converse with Adam and Eve in the Garden of Eden. The "cool of the day" may be in the beginning of the day or at the end of the day. Keep in mind that before there was central air conditioning, those living in hot climates used the cooler time of day for friendship with family and friends. As God's garden, most will find that the beginning or the end of the day is the best time for conversing with the Lord. And a great way to converse with the Lord is to discuss your day— what will happen or what did happen depending on when you pray, for the Lord loves to be involved in your day! Make Him a part of it by prayer.

There is another aspect of prayer that I want to compare to the two trees in the Garden of Eden. Just as there were two special trees in the Garden, there are two special types of prayer—prayer with the spirit and prayer with the understanding. The Apostle Paul instructed the church about this very issue.

> *For if I pray in a tongue, my spirit prays, but my understanding is unfruitful. What is the conclusion then? I will pray with the spirit, and I will also pray with the understanding. (1 Corinthians 14:14–15)*

Praying with the spirit is like partaking of the tree of life. Now, before I can continue my comparison, I must emphasize what does not compare—praying with the understanding does **not** compare to the tree of the knowledge of good and evil as it relates to God's commands. That is, He told Adam and Eve never to eat from that tree, but He tells us to pray always.[27] Praying with the understanding is in no way forbidden or evil.

Now I will continue my comparison of the two trees and prayer. Prayer with the understanding is like the tree of the knowledge of good and evil in the sense that we understand what we are praying about—good or evil things. To be exact, we are praying for or about good things; and at other times, we are praying about or against evil things. Prayer with the spirit (in tongues) is like the tree of life in the sense that we do not understand what we are praying; we just know it gives us life. The Scripture says it much better than I can in these verses:

> *And in the same way the Spirit is a help to our feeble hearts: for we are not able to make prayer to God in the right way; but the Spirit puts our desires into words which are not in our power to say;*
> *And he who is the searcher of hearts has knowledge of the mind of the Spirit, because he is making prayers for the saints in agreement with the mind of God. (Romans 8:26–27 BBE)*

---

[27] see 1 Thessalonians 5:17.

In my own personal prayer time, I pray for things with my understanding in order that I may know about what I'm praying. However, I spend a majority of my prayer time praying in tongues, which the Bible encourages us to do.[28] In fact, the Apostle Paul thanked God that he prayed in tongues more than anyone else did.[29]

Remember how the Scripture said that God *"took the man and gave him rest in the Garden of Eden in order to cultivate and watch over it."*[30] We are His garden and I have found that praying in tongues is like that—a rest for us, which cultivates and watches over our garden (our lives).

A third love cultivator is *worship*. Worship is much more than music and a song. Even so, singing to music is a vital element of worship. I believe God created music for the purpose of worship since music speaks to our spirit more than just words do. For sure, when you combine music with words of worship, it is easier to have an intense release of your emotions to God.

Interesting enough is the first warfare seen in the Garden of Eden—the war between the heavenly one created for worship (the serpent—Lucifer)[31] and the earthly one created for worship. The serpent won the first battle, but Jesus has won the war and now has an army of worshippers with more arising all the time!

---

[28] see Ephesians 6:18.
[29] see 1 Corinthians 14:18.
[30] see Genesis 2:15 TLV.
[31] see Isaiah 14:12–17 and Ezekiel 28:12–17.

God is searching for those who will worship Him in spirit and truth. Be His garden filled with the fragrance of worship!

Chapter Summary

Life in God's garden concerns the seeds and the growth—His words and our hearts. We are born again by His incorruptible seed.[32] There is nothing corrupt about His word, for true life and freedom are found when we willingly embrace all His words into our life.

He has given us two great "seeds"—the Bible and the still small voice—that inward voice of the Spirit. These two great seeds are not to be separated, for we need both the Bible and His Spirit for true life and freedom.[33] Just as it took God breathing His Spirit into Adam's nostrils for mankind to come alive, so it takes the Spirit of God to "breathe" on His word for it to come alive in us. The same is true of prayer and worship—we need to pray and worship with the spirit and with the understanding.

The ground is your heart and the most important part of it is your connection to His heart. This connection makes the ground soft and ready to receive the seed; for when you know how He feels about you, it prepares your heart for His seed. And the best way to plow up your ground (heart) is to know, to study, and to meditate on the beauty of God's personality. By doing this, it causes Him to become personally beautiful to you.

---

[32] see 1 Peter 1:23.
[33] see 2 Corinthians 3:6.

Think about this: Out of all of the wonders in the Garden of Eden, the highlight for Adam and Eve was God's love—His love for creation and His love for them. Nothing was more exhilarating for them than the love that God showed them. Then, in a moment, everything changed! They sinned. They feared. They hid. The joy they had felt at God's arrival in the Garden turned to fear even though God had not changed, which is shown in the fact that God came looking for them.

Then, about 4000 years later, a similar story is repeated with the opposite effect. In another garden, the Garden of Gethsemane, the last Adam (Jesus) embraced God's will, went to the cross, and finished His work. Then the curtain that separated man from God was torn in two—from top to bottom. God tore the curtain that kept us from Him so that we can now come boldly before Him even though we are completely naked before Him[34] (which Adam and Eve could not do).[35]

> So, friends, we can now—without hesitation —walk right up to God, into "the Holy Place." Jesus has cleared the way by the blood of his sacrifice, acting as our priest before God.
>
> . . . So let's do it—full of belief, confident that we're presentable inside and out. Let's keep a firm grip on the promises that keep us going. He always keeps his word. Let's see how inventive we can be in encouraging love and helping out, not avoiding worshiping together

---

34 see Hebrews 4:13.
35 see Genesis 3:10.

as some do but spurring each other on,
especially as we see the big Day
approaching. (Hebrews 10:19–25 TMSG)

In the next chapter, we will examine the two special trees in the Garden of Eden and see how they apply to our lives today.

Chapter 5

The Trees

The trees in the Garden of Eden were spectacular, each one a magnificent specimen. As Adam and Eve walked among them, something else was about to be revealed. . . .

In the center of the Garden, two trees held enormous power, a power unlike the other trees. These two trees had the power to change the destiny of Adam and Eve forever. Their response to these two trees would not only affect their destiny, but also the destiny of the Garden of Eden. Additionally, how they responded to these two trees would also affect the destiny of all of humanity forever. No other trees ever had such power as the two trees in the center of the Garden of Eden . . . *until there was a third tree with even greater power!*

In this chapter, we will look at these three trees in some detail while attempting to answer some interesting questions, such as: "What happened with the tree of the knowledge of good and evil?" "What happened to the tree of life?" "What happened to the Garden of Eden?"

As we look at each of these three trees, we will see that each one had importance in the Garden of Eden and in God's garden today. Our understanding of these trees will directly influence our life in His garden. Let's begin with the tree of the knowledge of good and evil.

The Tree of Knowledge

The tree of the knowledge of good and evil was a fruit tree. The fruit was extremely bad, or was it? Stay with me now as we examine this more closely.

Where did the tree of the knowledge of good and evil come from? According to most translations, God made it grow from the ground:

> *And out of the ground made the Lord God to grow **every tree** that is pleasant to the sight, and good for food; the tree of life also in the midst of the garden, and the tree of knowledge of good and evil. (Genesis 2:9 KJV emphasis added)*

A few translations make it sound as if God just placed the tree of knowledge of good and evil in the Garden. Nevertheless, the bottom line is that it came from God. The importance of this fact is seen in the following verse:

> *Then God saw everything that He had made, and indeed it was very good. (Genesis 1:31)*

Everything God made was very good! Adam and Eve were not flawed; neither was the tree of the knowledge of good and evil. I believe the tree was good and its fruit was good; however, God never intended for mankind to eat from this tree. In fact, He commanded them not to eat from it, and specifically told them what was good for food:

*And God said, "See, I have given you every
herb that yields seed which is on the face of
all the earth, and **every tree whose fruit
yields seed**; to you it shall be for food."
(Genesis 1:29 emphasis added)*

It appears from this verse that the fruit from the tree
of the knowledge of good did not have seeds within it.
Therefore, it was never given to mankind for food (thus,
the fruit was not an apple). It also appears that this tree
was never to reproduce and cause Adam and Eve, or
their decedents, to partake *accidentally* of a forbidden
fruit by not knowing where it came from. Therefore, if
mankind ever partook of the forbidden fruit it would not
be accidentally, but by willful disobedience to God.
Consequently, there was never to be any doubt about
which tree's fruit was forbidden.

I don't believe that the actual fruit that hung from
the tree was bad. In fact, Eve saw the fruit as something
good and looking delicious:

*When the woman saw that the fruit of the
tree was good for food and pleasing to the
eye . . . she took some and ate it. (Genesis 3:6
NIV)*

The tree's fruit was good, but the result of eating it
was extremely bad. In other words, the fruit itself was
good, but the "fruit" of eating it was disastrous!

So what caused the opening of their eyes to know
good and evil? Was it the fruit or the disobedience to
God? Obviously, it was the disobedience. Whether the

fruit had anything to do with it physically or not, sin is what opened their eyes. They went from being naked and not ashamed to being wide-eyed ashamed of their nakedness. They were not just naked before one another; they were naked before God.[1] This seemed to bring the most shame to them since they did not fully hide from each other (even though they had made covering for themselves); they hid *together* from God.

> *And they heard the sound of the Lord God*
> *walking in the garden in the cool of the day,*
> *and Adam and his wife hid themselves from*
> *the presence of the Lord God among the trees*
> *of the garden. (Genesis 3:8)*

This is one of the saddest moments in human history because they hid from the only One who could help them. I have often done the same thing when I have sinned and felt ashamed of my "naked condition" before God. I too have tried to cover over my "nakedness" with my own "fig-leaf-inventions" that never removed the shame. My "fig leaves" were usually trying extra hard to do good and not evil—so I wouldn't be ashamed before God—it never worked!

This is where we begin to see the *evilness of the good side* of the tree of knowledge of good and evil. They knew they needed their nakedness covered so they did something "good"—they made *themselves* coverings, which they knew to be a "good thing." But their good resulted in evil—they hid themselves from the presence of God! Why? Because ONLY the *goodness of God* can

---

[1] see Hebrews 4:13.

cover our nakedness and remove the evil in our heart by changing it.

> *Or do you despise the riches of His goodness, forbearance, and longsuffering, not knowing that the goodness of God leads you to repentance? (Romans 2:4)*

Our efforts to cover ourselves are an insult to God! How can this be? Is it not good for us to try to cover any evil in our hearts? No! It is not good; it is insulting! Ponder that for a moment because we have all done that very thing.

We insult God when we do not believe His goodness—His love for us. He *so loved us* that He gave His Son for us. John the Baptist said it best:

> *The next day John saw Jesus coming toward him, and said, "Behold! The Lamb of God who takes away the sin of the world!" (John 1:29)*

There is only one covering for our sin—the blood of Jesus. When we do not receive God's covering for our nakedness, but try to cover it with our good deeds, it is evil—it is sickening to God. Jesus said it this way:

> *"So then, because you are lukewarm, and neither cold nor hot, I will vomit you out of My mouth. **Because** you say, 'I am rich, have become wealthy, and have need of nothing'—and do not know that you are wretched, miserable, poor, blind, and*

> *naked—I counsel you to buy from **Me** . . .*
> *white garments, that you may be clothed,*
> *that the shame of your nakedness may not be*
> *revealed." (Revelation 3:16–18 emphasis*
> *added)*

God is so good that He became naked before us on the cross to remove the shame of our nakedness before Him. Without a doubt, the only remedy for our shame is to have God clothe our nakedness. Our coverings will never remove our shame. Therefore, Jesus was put to open shame on the cross to remove our shame.

> *Let us fix our eyes on Jesus, the author and*
> *perfecter of our faith, who for the joy set*
> *before him endured the cross, scorning its*
> *shame . . . (Hebrews 12:2 NIV)*

The meaning of the Greek word translated as *scorning* in the above verse is: *to think of with contempt or scorn, to despise, to refuse or reject something as wrong or disgraceful.* To say it another way, Jesus absolutely despises shame since it hinders His children from freely receiving His grace. That is, shame hinders us from coming with confidence before His throne of grace to find help in our time of need.[2]

Now that we know what Jesus thinks about shame, we may decide not to say to others, "Shame on you!"[3]

We now come to another interesting part concerning Eve's attitude about touching the tree of the knowledge

---

[2] see Hebrews 4:16.

[3] These last two paragraphs adapted from Steven J. Campbell, *The Christian's Bill of Rights*, Books for the Harvest, Farmington, 2012, pg. 25.

of good and evil, for it appears that God did not say that they could not touch the tree of the knowledge of good and evil. In fact, He put it right beside the tree of life in the middle of the Garden. Plus, all three times God repeats His command about the tree,[4] He never said that they could not *touch* the fruit since this could happen accidentally as they walked by the tree. However, Eve states that God commanded them not to touch it.[5] Why? I do not know, but by her adding to God's command it helped her to disobey instead of obey. How? Because before she ate the fruit, she touched it. And when she touched it, nothing happened—there was no death. Then the lies of the serpent (*"You will not surely die"* and *"in the day you eat of it your eyes will be opened, and you will be like God, knowing good and evil"*)[6] became more believable. Therefore, she was emboldened to go ahead and eat it.

Adding to God's commands is never a benefit for us; it never helps us not to sin. The Apostle Paul addressed this very issue:

> *Since you died with Christ to the basic principles of this world, why, as though you still belonged to it, do you submit to its rules: "Do not handle! Do not taste! Do not touch!"? These are all destined to perish with use, because they are based on human commands and teachings. Such regulations indeed have an appearance of wisdom, with their self-*

---

[4] see Genesis 2:17, 3:11, 3:17.
[5] see Genesis 3:3.
[6] see Genesis 3:4–5.

imposed worship, their false humility and their harsh treatment of the body, but they lack any value in restraining sensual indulgence. (Colossians 2:20–23 NIV)

Even if we think otherwise, human commands and teachings are of *no value* in restraining our sensual indulgence. Or as another translation states:

But they provide no help in conquering a person's evil desires. (Colossians 2:23 NLT)

Pride causes us to think we need to add to God's commands to keep ourselves pure. But Godlikeness never comes from us adding to our knowledge of good and evil, which is partaking of the wrong tree. Godlikeness can only come from partaking of true life— Jesus Christ, which is partaking of the right tree. As God's garden, the greatest choice you can make is to eat from the right tree and to cease eating from the wrong tree.

The tree of the knowledge of good and evil represents the fleshly aspect of us. Are we going to live by our own efforts to please God? Are we going to rely on our doing good and not evil? From which tree are we going to eat? One tree has us looking at ourselves; the other has us looking to God. When Adam and Eve partook of the tree of the knowledge of good and evil, they began to look at themselves. They began to judge what was good and evil about themselves and about one another. Then they hid from God!

Obviously, their knowledge of good and evil did not bring them closer to God. Neither will it help us.

Remember, knowledge of good and evil puffs up, but love builds up:

> *. . . we know that we all have knowledge. Knowledge puffs up, but love builds up. If anyone thinks he knows anything, he doesn't yet know as he ought to know. But if anyone loves God, he is known by Him.*
> *(1 Corinthians 8:1–3 TLV)*

When Adam and Eve were living from love, they enjoyed being close to God. When they began to live from their knowledge of good and evil, they hid from God. It is ironic that in the Garden the devil said, *"Eat from the tree and you will be like God;"* then after they did, he tells them, *"You can't be like God because you ate from the tree."* I believe this is what he said since this scenario is played out in our lives far too often. Many times, I have tried to gain God's approval by doing good and not evil, not realizing that I'm already accepted in Christ.[7] When I have fallen into this trap the devil was right there saying, "You're not good enough!" "You're too evil to be accepted by God."

Also, notice how God put good and evil together on the same tree; both were part of the forbidden fruit. The tree of the knowledge of good and evil produces fear—fear of who you are before God[8]—you believe you must hide from God because you have done evil.

At other times, we think we will be closer to God because of our knowledge of good and evil instead of

---

7 see Ephesians 1:6.
8 see Genesis 3:10.

realizing we are only close to God by our life in Christ.[9]
Our knowledge may puff us up (pride), which causes
God to resist us;[10] whereas humility causes us to look to
what Christ has already done for us—in Him we live and
move and have our being.[11]

Again, I want to emphasize an important point about
the tree of the knowledge of good and evil. The
knowledge of *good* was part of the forbidden fruit! Many
miss this very important point. So why was the
knowledge of good forbidden also? Because of what it
produced in mankind. Let me explain this truth.

The first "good" action Adam and Eve took after
sinning was to make loin-coverings. They knew that it
was good to be covered. What is wrong with that? They
felt they were not good enough to be in God's presence,
so they tried to look good instead of looking to God to
help them. I too have fallen into that same trap too
many times.

Furthermore, the "good side" of the tree of the
knowledge of good and evil helped Cain to kill Abel.
How? Cain *knew* that Abel's offering was *good* and
acceptable to God but his offering was not good enough
to be accepted by God. This made Cain very angry with
God and with Abel. Cain's jealousy of his brother's
goodness caused him to murder Abel even though God
Himself tried to curb Cain's anger.[12]

Too often, my knowledge of what is good has caused
me to look at another and criticize him or her. Why?

9 see Romans chapters 7 and 8 for more on this subject.
10 see 1 Peter 5:5.
11 see Acts 17:28.
12 see Genesis 4:6.

Because I didn't think they were being good enough, at least not according to my standards. At this point, I highly recommend reading Romans 1:18–2:16 and James chapter 3. These Scriptures usually convict me of my own tendency to criticize others instead of examining my own heart to see why their actions bother me.

Now we come to something not easy to explain, but vital to understand—the wickedness of the knowledge of good and evil. How is it wicked? It is wicked because it usurps the lordship of Christ; it is mankind attempting to be like God apart from God. Thus, God prohibited humans from reaching out and taking the knowledge of good and evil as their own, for only God was to be the source of the knowledge of good and evil because humans were created to live under His authority, His lordship.

To see this, just look at what happened when mankind rejected God's authority and chose to partake of the knowledge of good and evil. Immediately, they began to determine what was good and what was evil, and with the devil gaining authority in the earth,[13] humans quickly gravitated toward evil. Only a few gravitated toward God's authority—His knowledge of good and evil.

The problem with humanity's knowledge of good and evil is that each person has their own perceptions of good and evil that they try to live by and often try to get others to live by. *Only* through God's authority is there ONE standard of good and evil—God's. Only as we live

---

[13] see 2 Corinthians 4:4.

under His lordship do we live righteously, which is where we see the importance of following the Holy Spirit, who always leads us to follow God's Word—the Bible.

However, this does not mean that we will all see or think the same about good and evil. Why? Because the knowledge of God and His ways is a growth and we are all at different levels of growth and understanding. But with *one* standard of good and evil, we can all head in the same direction.

To say all this in another way, we do the good we do because God said to do it—we do it to please Him. Also, we don't do evil things because God said not to do them—to please Him, we don't do them. As Lord, He is the ruling force in our lives; He is our knowledge of good and evil.

You may want to meditate on the next few sentences as I apply what I am saying to our lives concerning how we speak to others. That is, we should not just tell others what is good and evil for them; we should tell them what **Jesus says** is good and evil for them. In doing this, they will be confronted with Jesus' authority and not just what they would perceive as our opinion, but they will be confronted with His lordship over their lives.

To believe that Jesus Christ is Lord is to believe that He alone has the authority to say what is good and evil in a person's life. Even so, He has given us the responsibility to speak into the lives of others; however, we should only do it under His authority—by His Spirit. For God will give you authority to speak into the lives of those you love. It is true that the more you love someone, the more authority you will have to speak into his or her life.

At this time, the fruit of the tree of knowledge of good and evil is coming to maturity and with that, knowledge seems to be the most valuable product on earth. However, it is extremely flawed in many areas. Consequently, as human knowledge of good and evil comes to maturity, it results in calling good evil and evil good.[14] There are many examples of this in the world today. One example would be pro-choice and pro-life, for there are many who call pro-lifers evil and abortionists good.

Calling evil good began with the devil in the Garden of Eden when he made evil sound good. He said that if they ate from the tree nothing bad would happen but they would be like God and have new wisdom. However, God said:

> But of the fruit of the tree of the knowledge of good and evil you may not take; for **on the day** when you take of it, death will certainly come to you. (Genesis 2:17 BBE emphasis added)

According to God's statement above, Adam and Eve would physically die on the very day that they ate from the tree of the knowledge of good and evil. Do you realize that this is exactly what happened? Both Adam and Eve were buried before the day ended! What? How could that be true? I will show you from the Scriptures.

---

[14] see Isaiah 5:20.

First, keep in mind that God sees and thinks differently than we do as shown in the following verses:

> *"My thoughts are nothing like your*
> *thoughts," says the Lord.*
> *"And my ways are far beyond anything*
> *you could imagine.*
> *For just as the heavens are higher than the*
> *earth, so my ways are higher than your*
> *ways and my thoughts higher than your*
> *thoughts." (Isaiah 55:8–9 NLT)*

So how did God see Adam and Eve as physically dying on the same day that they sinned? Peter tells us in the following verse:

> *But, my loved ones, keep in mind this one*
> *thing, that with the Lord one day is the same*
> *as a thousand years, and **a thousand***
> ***years are no more than one day.***
> *(2 Peter 3:8 BBE emphasis added)*

Adam and Eve both died before a thousand years had transpired. Thus, they both died the same day that they sinned!—at least from God's perspective. Since all have sinned and **"on the day** when you take of it, death will certainly come to you,"[15] this could be the reason why no early human being was able to live more than a thousand years—more than one day from God's viewpoint. Yes, they came close but never lived over a thousand years. Adam lived more than 900 years; and during his lifetime, he saw many people die. We can

---

[15] Genesis 2:17 BBE emphasis added.

only imagine how Adam felt as he saw the first person die, and then another, and another, and another— knowing that he caused all the death.

> *... For the sin of this one man, Adam, brought death to many. (Romans 5:15 NLT)*

As you probably know, the first person to die in the Bible was Adam's son Abel. And he did not just die; he was murdered—and it gets even worse—he was murdered by his brother Cain, Adam's firstborn son. How did this make Adam feel? Surely he felt the depth of his sin as its effect took hold of all human beings, even his firstborn son—who became a murderer.

Everywhere Adam looked, humans were entering into sin, and death was spreading like wildfire. Oh, how he must have longed for God to come and annul all he had done through his sin.

As parents, Adam and Eve saw all too quickly their sin spread to all their descendents. This had to hurt them deeply. How do I know that? Because, as a parent, I hurt deeply when my sin, weakness, or brokenness was duplicated in my children. To see them do the very thing that I should not do was when the ugliness of my action hit me hard because I saw my sin, weakness, or brokenness more accurately when it was reflected in my children.

No doubt, Adam and Eve saw the ugliness of their sin as it was reflected in humanity. However, God is so kind and so merciful that I believe He showed Adam and Eve at least some of His plan of redemption, He may have shown them some of the following:

But there is a great difference between Adam's sin and God's gracious gift. For the sin of this one man, Adam, brought death to many. But even greater is God's wonderful grace and his gift of forgiveness to many through this other man, Jesus Christ. And the result of God's gracious gift is very different from the result of that one man's sin. For Adam's sin led to condemnation, but God's free gift leads to our being made right with God, even though we are guilty of many sins. For the sin of this one man, Adam, caused death to rule over many. But even greater is God's wonderful grace and his gift of righteousness, for all who receive it will live in triumph over sin and death through this one man, Jesus Christ.

Yes, Adam's one sin brings condemnation for everyone, but Christ's one act of righteousness brings a right relationship with God and new life for everyone. Because one person disobeyed God, many became sinners. But because one other person obeyed God, many will be made righteous. (Romans 5:15–19 NLT)

Oh, how Jesus must have felt knowing that He would be the source of all the grace and life released to humanity through His cross. Truly, this was the joy set before Him as He was on the cross. As the Scripture states, *"Jesus, the author and finisher of our faith, who*

for the joy that was set before Him endured the
cross" (Hebrews 12:2 emphasis added).

By the way, where were Adam and Eve at when the
serpent tempted them? Were they already looking at the
two trees, comparing them? Were they wondering what
the difference was? We do not know, but they were in a
prime location to be tempted.

> *Let no one say when he is tempted, "I am
> tempted by God"; for God cannot be tempted
> by evil, nor does He Himself tempt anyone.
> But each one is tempted when he is drawn
> away by his own desires and enticed. Then,
> when desire has conceived, it gives birth to
> sin; and sin, when it is full-grown, brings
> forth death. (James 1:13–15)*

The tree of the knowledge of good and evil was not in
the midst of the Garden of Eden to tempt mankind; God
allowed the devil in the Garden for that purpose. The
temptation was allowed to prove Adam and Eve's
worthiness to rule over the earth—that they would rule
under God's authority and not just their own authority—
that their will would be subject to His will. For that
reason, the devil was allowed in the Garden to tempt
them—to prove them. However, the first Adam failed
the test; it took the last Adam (Jesus) to pass the test.

Up to the time of sin, mankind did not know evil or
good. They had done nothing evil; they had done
nothing "good" either. They simply yielded to the life in
them, doing what they were created to do. They were
not performing, not doing "good"; they were just living

the life God gave them to live with all its duties. We are called to do the same—to simply yield to the life within us—the Holy Spirit.[16] In fact, Jesus told us what our attitude should be:

> *"And does the master thank the servant for doing what he was told to do? Of course not. In the same way, when you obey me you should say, 'We are unworthy servants who have simply done our duty.'" (Luke 17:9–10 NLT)*

Now let's start to answer the question we asked at the beginning of this chapter, "What happened with the tree of the knowledge of good and evil?"

First, since the Bible does not directly answer the question, we cannot say for sure what happened to this tree. However, since we live in a technological age, you can easily search on the Internet and find various theories. A popular theory is that it was destroyed in the flood of Noah's day. On the other hand, there may be another possibility recorded in Scripture, for I believe it is a real possibility that Ezekiel alludes to the tree of the knowledge of good and evil in chapter 31 as he did allude to Satan in chapter 28. If you are not familiar with this, Ezekiel gives a word to the king of Tyre in chapter 28, but he says, *"You were in Eden, the garden of God."* Therefore, many believe Ezekiel is speaking of Satan and not just the king of Tyre who had the spirit of Satan working in him.

---

[16] see Romans 8:1–17.

Then we come to chapter 31 where Ezekiel speaks to Pharaoh king of Egypt who is likened to a great tree. I believe the same thing applies here—that Ezekiel alludes to the tree of the knowledge of good and evil when he speaks of Egypt as a great tree. Also, keep in mind that Egypt represented bondage and slavery for God's people Israel, which is what the tree of the knowledge of good and evil introduced—bondage and slavery for all of humanity.[17]

Now, let's first look at this portion of Ezekiel's allegory:

> *"The cedar trees in the garden of God*
> *were not as great as it was. . . .*
> *No tree in the garden of God*
> *was as beautiful as this tree.*
> *I made it beautiful with many branches,*
> *and all the trees of Eden in the garden of*
> *God wanted to be like it." (Ezekiel 31:8–9*
> *NCV)*

If this alludes to the tree of the knowledge of good and evil and *if* Ezekiel is still alluding to it in the next verse, then here is what happened to the tree of the knowledge of good and evil:

> *"'So this is what the Lord God says: The tree*
> *grew tall. Its top reached the clouds, and it*
> *became proud of its height. So I handed it*
> *over to a mighty ruler of the nations for him*
> *to punish it. Because it was evil, I got rid of*

---

[17] see John 8:34.

it. The cruelest foreign nation cut it down and left it. The tree's branches fell on the mountains and in all the valleys, and its broken limbs were in all the ravines of the land. . . .'" (Ezekiel 31:10–13 NCV)

As Ezekiel continues to talk about Pharaoh king of Egypt in the next verses, I believe he is still alluding to the tree of the knowledge of good and evil. I will highlight a few of the verses here:

"'This is what the Lord God says: On the day when the tree went down to the place of the dead . . . Then all the trees of Eden . . . were comforted in the place of the dead below the earth. These trees had also gone down with the great tree to the place of the dead. . . .

"'So no tree in Eden is equal to you, Egypt, in greatness and honor, but you will go down to join the trees of Eden in the place below the earth. . . .'" (Ezekiel 31:15–18 NCV)

(NOTE: *Sheol* is translated as "the place of the dead" in the above verses. This is an excellent translation of the word *Sheol* as it means *the place, or realm of the dead.* Both the righteous and wicked entered Sheol at death, one comforted, and one in torment.[18] It would be to your benefit to study the subject of Sheol/Hades, which I cannot do here since it is beyond the scope of this book.)

---

[18] see Luke 16:19–31.

As stated earlier, this is my opinion of what happened to the tree of knowledge **IF** Ezekiel is alluding to it in these verses. I think he is, but I leave it up to the reader to make his or her own judgment.

Furthermore, I think it is possible that the very nature of the tree of the knowledge of good and evil changed at the same time as Adam and Eve's nature changed after they sinned. Just as the tree that Ezekiel speaks of grew immense, so humanity's knowledge of good and evil grew quickly. The *first* two sons of Adam and Eve show this very thing—Abel was righteous (good) and Cain was a murderer (evil).

It is possible that the tree of the knowledge of good and evil grew along with humanity's knowledge of good and evil. In other words, the more humanity's knowledge of good and evil grew, the more the tree grew. Thus, God may have waited to destroy the tree of the knowledge of good and evil until at (or near) the time of the Great Flood. I see this as a real possibility.

I have written enough about this tree since life in God's garden, your life, is about freedom from the bondage of this tree. Also, please keep in mind that whatever God says you can't do is to keep you free. Remember, Jesus set the example of how to walk in freedom—simply listen and obey your *loving heavenly Father!* Now let's get to the next two trees that are life-giving trees.

The Tree of Life

In writing about the tree of life, I was surprised about how little I knew about it, as I had assumed several things about this tree that I do not believe now. Also, I think that as I share some obvious observations about the tree, the unexplained nature of this tree will become apparent.

Let's start with a most obvious fact about the Garden of Eden; it was FULL of life. It seemed everything had life. Some things could sustain life (good for food) and others, including animals, had the ability to reproduce life (seeds). But something was so special about this one tree that it was called *the tree of life*. No other tree in the Garden was called a tree of life—a tree that gives life. Therefore, the clear fact is that this unique tree can give life, which is the obvious reason for God putting the tree of life in the Garden of Eden—to give, or sustain life in a special way (for those who partook of it).

But here is where the obvious is not so obvious. If Adam and Eve were never going to die (unless they sinned) what was the purpose of the tree of life? It was not to give life; they already had life. And it certainly wasn't there to give them life in case they sinned, for God made sure they could never partake of the tree of life after they sinned. The only other purpose I see for the tree would be to sustain life, to be like the oxygen and the food that God provided, which mankind needed to sustain their life. However, the problem I see with this is the strength of the power of the tree of life since it appears to have more power than just sustaining life. For God said that the tree of life had the power for humankind to live forever by partaking of it.

> *Then the Lord God said, "Look, the human beings have become like us, knowing both*

*good and evil. What if they reach out, take
fruit from the tree of life, and eat it? Then
they will live forever!" (Genesis 3:22 NLT)*

The tree of life had more power than the power of
death that the tree of the knowledge of good and evil
had—at least physically. Just by eating from the tree of
life, the power of physical death would be overcome.
Therefore, it is reasonable to assume that Adam and Eve
never ate from the tree of life for if they did, the power
of the tree of life would have overcome the power of
physical death (but Adam died at 930 years old).[19]

I see this as true unless the previous verse required a
regular monthly eating and not just eating once for them
to live forever. If that is the case, then I see how it is
possible that Adam and Eve could have partaken of the
tree of life and still died. I do not think this is what
happened, but I mention this because of what this
Scripture says:

*The Tree of Life was planted on each side of
the River, producing twelve kinds of fruit, a
ripe fruit each month. (Revelation 22:2
TMSG)*

Assuming that Adam and Eve never ate from the tree
of life, I ask this question, "Why would they not have
partaken of the tree of life since God said they could
freely eat of it?"[20] Maybe they simply did not see the
need for it since they never felt they were dying or saw
any death around them. Plus, they had many other trees

---

[19] see Genesis 5:5.
[20] see Genesis 2:16.

to eat from that God gave to *sustain* their life. (Yes, Adam and Eve had to breathe and eat to sustain their life, for God made humans that way.)

But this raises another question, "Why would God have a tree of life in the midst of the Garden of Eden if it was never used?" I have a simple answer, "I do not know!" Simply put, I have found many things about the tree of life to be unexplained. However, I do want to point out that we may find some answers by looking at ourselves. Remember, I have shown from the Scriptures that we are called God's garden. As God's garden, we have been given a "tree of life" in the baptism of the Holy Spirit. Even so, some have never seen the need to partake of this "tree of life." Others have partaken once (spoken in tongues once) but never again. Still others partake regularly of this "tree of life." (Just to be clear, I am *not* saying that the Holy Spirit or speaking in tongues is the tree of life in the Garden of Eden.)

Sad to say, I have had times in my life where I have gone for days without speaking in tongues; I was too self-reliant, not realizing my need for the life God placed in my midst (His garden). The Holy Spirit is a *river of LIFE*; I should never dam it up by not letting Him flow out of me.[21]

As our "tree of life," the Holy Spirit even gives life to our mortal bodies.

> *But if the Spirit of Him who raised Jesus from the dead dwells in you, He who raised Christ from the dead will also give life to*

---

[21] see John 7:38–39.

*your mortal bodies through His Spirit who
dwells in you. (Romans 8:11)*

Just as God invited Adam and Eve to eat freely from
the trees, He freely invites all to receive the baptism of
the Holy Spirit:

> *Peter said, "Change your life. Turn to God
> and be baptized, each of you, in the name of
> Jesus Christ, so your sins are forgiven.
> Receive the gift of the Holy Spirit. The
> promise is targeted to you and your
> children, but also to all who are far away—
> whomever, in fact, our Master God invites."
> (Acts 2:38–39 TMSG)*

I did not receive the baptism of the Holy Spirit when
I was born again. It was over a year later, after I heard
God's invitation from the Scriptures, that I received the
baptism of the Holy Spirit with speaking in tongues.

In my life, I have found speaking in tongues to be a
"tree of life." In fact, a very large portion of my prayer
time is spent praying in tongues. Through His grace, I
have seen the importance of partaking of this "tree of
life" on a daily basis, but not all see their need to partake
of this "tree of life," just as I did not see my need for
several months.

The early church knew the power of this "tree of life"
and prayed for believers to receive the baptism of the
Holy Spirit with speaking in tongues.[22] The Apostle Paul
even tells us how much he prayed in tongues—more

---

[22] see Acts 19:1–6.

than anyone did![23] Could this be a major reason for Paul's fruitful life? I believe so. For Paul (Saul) had a deep knowledge of the Word of God but bore little, if any, fruit. Then when he received Jesus and the baptism of the Holy Spirit and prayed in tongues more than anyone else did, his life became very fruitful. This is because the Word of God needs the Spirit of God and the Spirit of God needs the Word of God to produce abundant fruit in a life. I will cover more about this in the next chapter, but if you want to be a very fruitful garden, it requires God's Word and God's Spirit. To say it another way, you need to partake of the Word of God and the baptism of the Holy Spirit daily to produce *abundant* fruit.

I believe the Holy Spirit is our source of life—a "tree of life" for us. We are to live from this "tree" within us— the Holy Spirit.

The following is just one of my ideas of why God placed the tree of life in the Garden of Eden. Keep in mind that we all see in part and know in part;[24] therefore, you probably have a better idea than mine. Even so, here is a possibility I see.

The purpose of the two trees in the midst of the Garden of Eden was to learn to make right choices—to learn obedience, to love the right choice and hate the evil choice—to be like Jesus, who loved righteousness and hated evil.[25]

---

[23] see 1 Corinthians 14:18.

[24] see 1 Corinthians 13:9.

[25] see Hebrews 1:9.

As I stated in an earlier chapter, the two trees in the midst of the Garden were for learning to manage free will.[26] As free will agents, God puts choices before us—life and death so that we may freely choose life![27]

As God's garden, there are always choices before you. Are you going to follow his path for your life or make your own path? Your life in God's garden is a series of choices, therefore, choose life!

We can only manage free will by yielding to the Holy Spirit. However, it is beyond the scope of this book to go into detail about this except to recommend a careful reading of Romans chapter 8.

I now want to present a question I have had, "What happened to the tree of life?" Just as with the tree of the knowledge of good and evil, God does not directly tell us what happened to the tree of life. So again, my answer is simple, "I do not know!"

Even so, I do want to present an idea that I have about what happened to the tree of life. It is my idea; so don't be surprised when you get to heaven and find out that my idea was not even close.

First, I want to point out that I do not believe that the tree was contaminated by Adam's sin since it kept its power after his sin, so much so that God had to keep mankind from its power; because God did not want unredeemed humanity receiving of its power and living forever. How long God guarded the tree of life we do not know, but it was guarded until God did something with it.

---

[26] see page 41–42.
[27] see Deuteronomy 30:19.

Also, keep in mind that around the tree of life God placed Cherubim, which are the ones that magnify the holiness and power of God and watch over holy things (such as the mercy seat on the Ark of the Covenant)— another reason why I believe that the tree of life remained holy. So what did God do with the tree of life? Again, this is just my speculation, but if the tree of life was not included with the trees Ezekiel spoke of in chapter 31, then I think it may have been transplanted to heaven after a time just as Enoch was translated to heaven. And **IF** the tree of life was transplanted to heaven, then it could be one of the trees spoken of in this verse:

> *And he showed me a pure river of water of life, clear as crystal, proceeding from the throne of God and of the Lamb. In the middle of its street, and on either side of the river, was the tree of life, which bore twelve fruits, **each tree** yielding its fruit every month. (Revelation 22:1–2 emphasis added)*

Could it be that one of these trees was originally in heaven and the other one originally in the Garden of Eden? (Not all translations seem to agree that there are two trees; some seem to indicate there is just one tree that had its growth on both sides of the river. But I wonder if just as God is one God in three Persons, the tree of life could be one tree in two plants.) Whatever the case, it is interesting to note that although mankind was kept from the tree of life in the Garden of Eden, Jesus promises us access to the tree of life in God's paradise, if we overcome:

"He who has an ear, let him hear what the Spirit says to the churches. To him who overcomes I will give to eat from the tree of life, which is in the midst of the Paradise of God." (Revelation 2:7)

I will end this section with one last question, "Whatever happened to the Garden of Eden?" "Did it just disappear or degenerate into something else when, or if, the tree of life was taken?" I would guess that it went the way of the tree of the knowledge of good and evil.

I now want to turn our attention to the greatest of all trees.

The Greatest Tree

Trees are one of the greatest of God's creations. In fact, they play a key role in sustaining life on earth because they are a major part of the Carbon Dioxide–Oxygen Cycle that sustains life. That is, they take in carbon dioxide and give off oxygen that the animal kingdom breathes in to breathe out carbon dioxide that the trees take in—another amazing way God created life on the earth.

Out of all of the trees, there were only three trees with the power to affect eternal destinies. We looked at the first two and now come to the third tree that is the greatest of all trees. This tree has the power to restore all things; it has the power to overcome *all* the aspects of sin and death!

Though Adam and Eve may not have seen the value or need to partake of the tree of life before they sinned, no doubt that changed as they experienced the effects of their disobedience. Then, though they surely wanted to partake of the tree of life, God had the Cherubim and a flaming sword preventing it. Even so, God still desired to enjoy humanity as at the first, but this became increasingly impossible; for even if they would have been allowed to eat from the tree of life after sin, it would not have restored the Garden of Eden nor God's garden (mankind). As a result, instead of God enjoying human beings, they pained His heart:

> *The LORD was grieved that he had made man on the earth, and his heart was filled with pain. So the LORD said, "I will wipe mankind, whom I have created, from the face of the earth—men and animals ... —for I am grieved that I have made them." But Noah found favor in the eyes of the LORD. (Genesis 6:6–8 NIV)*

This is one of the saddest portions of Scripture because humans pained the heart of God. Instead of God enjoying His creation, He was going to have to destroy them.

So what kind of tree did it take to restore humanity, to restore God's enjoyment of them? It took a more powerful tree of life; it took a tree infused with the greatest power in the universe—love. Therefore, since God wanted full fellowship with mankind restored, His love was uncovered upon a tree—the cross.

Jesus' blood oozed on and into the cross, which became our "tree of life." To clarify, the "tree" is not the source of life; but *His life given up* while on the cross is our "tree of life." The blood Jesus shed on the cross is our "tree of life" since the life is in the blood.[28] Jesus confirmed this with these words:

> *"I am the living bread that came down from heaven. Anyone who eats this bread will live forever; and this bread, which I will offer so the world may live, is my flesh."*
>
> *Then the people began arguing with each other about what he meant. "How can this man give us his flesh to eat?" they asked.*
>
> *So Jesus said again, "I tell you the truth, unless you eat the flesh of the Son of Man and drink his blood, you cannot have eternal life within you. But anyone who eats my flesh and drinks my blood has eternal life, and I will raise that person at the last day. For my flesh is true food, and my blood is true drink. Anyone who eats my flesh and drinks my blood remains in me, and I in him. I live because of the living Father who sent me; in the same way, anyone who feeds on me will live because of me. (John 6:51–57 NLT)*

The most dreadful force humans knew (death) was totally defeated by the cross! By Jesus sacrificing His life, our fear of death was defeated. Specifically, when

---

[28] see Leviticus 17:11.

the Holy Spirit raised Jesus from the dead the fear of death was defeated.[29]

The tree mankind needed to become God's garden again was the cross. Through the cross, God could delight in humanity again, which does not mean that He did not delight in anyone before the cross; it simply means that the saints of the Old Testament could be enjoyed by God because of the Lamb of God (Jesus) who was to come.

The Bible often refers to the cross as a tree.[30] And it was on this tree that the true-deep-knowledge of God was and is revealed. While the devil said that you could be like God by knowing good and evil; God says that you can only be like Him by knowing Him. This begins at the cross, for the cross reveals God and gives us the power to be like Him.[31] Whereas the knowledge of good and evil puts a veil on our hearts, the cross lifts the veil.[32] It was the love of God shown on the cross that ripped the veil from top to bottom. No doubt, it was to let humans into God's presence, but another part you don't want to miss seeing is that it let God out! It let God's heart be totally exposed—He is love!

This love is not abstract; it is very personal—He loves YOU so much! He visibly displayed His love for you on the cross as His very own Son suffered and died for *you!* The cross, while a most horrible sight is the most glorious sight for you—the passionate love of God for you put on public display.

[29] see Hebrews 2:14–15.
[30] see Acts 5:30, 10:39, 13:29, 1 Peter 2:24, etc.
[31] see Hebrews 12:1–4.
[32] see 2 Corinthians 3:12–18.

A part of what Jesus meant with His words, *"It is finished!"* is that the heart of God is forever revealed. The following is verses one and three of an old hymn called *The Love of God* that fittingly speaks of His love for us.

The love of God is greater far
Than tongue or pen can ever tell;
It goes beyond the highest star,
And reaches to the lowest hell;
The guilty pair, bowed down with care,
God gave His Son to win;
His erring child He reconciled,
And pardoned from his sin.

Refrain:
O love of God, how rich and pure!
How measureless and strong!
It shall forevermore endure
The saints' and angels' song.

Could we with ink the ocean fill,
And were the skies of parchment made,
Were every stalk on earth a quill,
And every man a scribe by trade,
To write the love of God above,
Would drain the ocean dry.
Nor could the scroll contain the whole,
Though stretched from sky to sky.

—Frederick M. Lehman, 1917
—verse 3 by Meir Ben Isaac Nehorai, 1050

Through God's love and mercy, we go from God forbidding eating from the tree of life to Him bidding all to come to His "tree of life"—the cross. The cross has the power to give eternal life *spiritually* and physically. It is a greater tree than the tree of life that could only give physical life.

Even as a tree was used to cause the fall of mankind into sin and death, God used a tree to sacrifice His Son to redeem us from sin and death. Interestingly enough, both of these things took place in or very near a garden.

> *Now in the place where He was crucified there was a garden, and in the garden a new tomb in which no one had yet been laid. So there they laid Jesus, because of the Jews' Preparation Day, for the tomb was nearby. (John 19:41–42)*

After Jesus died, He was placed in a garden. He rose from the dead in a garden! The power of death that began in a garden was defeated in a garden!

Before sin, humanity was created to experience the garden-type environment. After sin, humanity was expelled from the garden-type atmosphere. However, as a new creation in Christ through the cross, we will be expelled from this present garden-less atmosphere into the paradise of God—the garden-type atmosphere of heaven. But sad to say, those still in their sins go into a worse realm with not even a hint of a garden-type atmosphere.

God seems to love contrast. He separated light from dark, day from night, and water from dry land. He put the tree of life next to the tree of the knowledge of good and evil. He used a tree to redeem us from the fall when a tree was used to cause the fall. Also, while nakedness caused man to hide from God after partaking of the forbidden tree; Jesus hung naked on a tree to open wide the heart of God's acceptance of humanity drawing them to Himself with His naked love. There are many other contrasts in Scripture, such as, *"For the wages of sin is death, but the gift of God is eternal life in Christ Jesus our Lord."*[33]

In Summary

It seems as though all three of these trees in this chapter are "alive" today fighting for our attention, trying to get us to partake of them. I liken these three trees to the following:

The tree of the knowledge of good and evil— religion—trying to have the good outweigh the bad in our life—to be good enough to get into heaven. There is no true life in this tree.

The tree of life—physical life—only being concerned with present comfort—doing anything to save our life. This results in losing true life.[34]

The cross—spiritual and physical life—not satisfied, but always pressing on to obtain all the cross procured— hungering and thirsting for righteousness—seeing the goodness and severity of God[35]—seeing God as love *and* as a consuming fire. Because of the cross, we see our need for holiness.

---

[33] see Romans 6:23 and 5:12–21.
[34] see Luke 9:24.
[35] see Romans 11:22.

Make every effort to live in peace with all men and to be holy; without holiness no one will see the Lord. (Hebrews 12:14 NIV)

Holiness can only come through the cross—through Jesus by the power of the Holy Spirit.

In the next chapter, I will show you an incredible thing—humans can give God (the One already perfect in glory) great glory.

Chapter 6

The Fruit

L ife in God's garden is full of purpose. Having written about several of the purposes already, the next two chapters will focus on the *central* purpose of life in God's garden. In doing this, I hope that your heart will come alive in a greater way as you see more of the purpose of your life—to bear fruit.

Let's begin at the beginning—the Garden of Eden. Very shortly after God creates man, He places him in the Garden.[1] In the Garden, man begins to experience life— life with God. As the first human, Adam begins to take pleasure in the greatest aspect of life—fellowship with God! Their fellowship began around God's creation that He brought to Adam to name:

> *So the Lord God formed from the ground all the wild animals and all the birds of the sky. He brought them to the man to see what he would call them, and the man chose a name for each one. He gave names to all the livestock, all the birds of the sky, and all the wild animals. (Genesis 2:19–20 NLT)*

I want you to take time with me now to absorb these Scriptures and let's use our imagination to see just what

---

[1] see Genesis 2:8.

happened here. I believe that God so enjoyed showing Adam each of His creatures that He brought each animal individually before Adam instead of all the animals at once; and as each animal was introduced to Adam, I think each creature "showed-off" how God made him or her special. This experience was very enjoyable for God, for Adam, and the creature before them. Then out of this enjoyable time together, Adam was able to accurately name each animal, which began mankind's enjoyable time with God and His creation.

During this time, Adam began to know God as a loving creator and a great fellowship arose between God, man, and His creation. This fellowship grew over time— the time it took to name *all* the birds of the sky, *all* the livestock, and *all* of the wild animals.

Now, I want to look at what I think happened as God brought the animals to Adam to name. To begin with, I don't think God brought just an individual animal before Adam; I think He brought each kind of animal individually as a pair—male and female. Why is this significant? Because one of the first lessons God was giving Adam is that He makes males and females, which is good and right.

I believe God enjoyed showing Adam the unique characteristics of each gender of each animal, which caused Adam to be in awe of his most-creative God. That is, Adam would marvel as God revealed the uniqueness of the male and female of each animal.

God is so intentional in what He does; by bringing the animals to Adam as male and female, He was imparting into Adam knowledge—knowledge from God about what is good. The significance of this is three-fold.

First, it showed that knowledge from God is good, but the fruit of knowledge apart from God is evil, for again, we are seeing why God forbid mankind from partaking of the knowledge of good and evil apart from Him—getting it their own way. Because in recent times, as the fruit of the tree of the knowledge of good and evil is coming to maturity, more and more people are saying it is good for a person to choose their gender; that it is evil to assign a gender to someone because of how they look [how God created them]. They are pushing for every person to choose what gender they want to be—to take the authority of choosing their gender away from God. In this, we see yet again the result of mankind obtaining knowledge apart from God.

Second, as God brought all the animals to Adam so that they could experience His creation together, something began to take place—Adam's heart became more interwoven to God's heart. How? Adam saw that each of the animals had a mate comparable to them, which opened his eyes to the most important lesson of all—God was his companion! He was created for God!

Third, keep in mind that God brought ALL the animals to Adam to name, which took a considerable amount of time. Knowing that God is never hurried, and the number of animals to name (possibly thousands); I cannot see it taking less than a year. Also, Adam did not just arbitrarily pick out a name, but he observed the animals closely before naming each one. Thinking about the time this took, I am reminded of what God said in Deuteronomy 24:5:

> *"When a man has taken a new wife, he shall not go out to war or be charged with any business; he shall be free at home one year, and bring happiness to his wife whom he has taken."*

Could it be that God Himself wanted at least a year to establish His relationship with Adam for "bringing happiness" (pleasure and fulfillment) to both of them through their relationship? I believe that is exactly what happened!

By Adam spending at least the first year of his life alone with God, it shows that we are created to be His garden. Remember the definition I gave for a garden: *a well-defined area made for the pleasure and/or fulfillment of the one designing it and for the one(s) who will enjoy it.* We are His garden and the purpose of being His garden is for His pleasure and fulfillment in us, and for our pleasure and fulfillment in Him.

Each day was a new experience for Adam as God brought more of His creatures to him to name and become a part of the Garden of Eden. As God's garden today, we too can have new experiences every day.

> *Because of the Lord's great love we are not*
> *consumed, for his compassions never fail.*
> *They are new every morning;*
> *great is your faithfulness.*
> *(Lamentations 3:22–23 NIV)*

Life in God's garden should be new and exciting every day, at least for the most part. Certainly, we will all have days that are not exciting. Every person in the Bible had those days and we will too. Even Jesus had the day when He had to endure extreme suffering and then death on the cross. Yes, He found a joy in it because of what it was accomplishing, but His flesh suffered. We too can count our sufferings as joy knowing what is being produced in us.

> *Dear brothers and sisters, when troubles come your way, consider it an opportunity for great joy. For you know that when your faith is tested, your endurance has a chance to grow. So let it grow, for when your endurance is fully developed, you will be perfect and complete, needing nothing.* (*James 1:2–4 NLT*)

Furthermore, I see God having this "year" alone with Adam as the reason why He changed His usual creation method of creating the male and female at the same time. That is, by not creating Eve at the same time as Adam, God had time alone with him. In doing this, God is showing us that mankind is first created for relationship with God before relationship with others, even a spouse. At this point, I would highly recommend reading 1 Corinthians chapter 7. I will only quote a few verses here:

> *I want you to be free from the concerns of this life. An unmarried man can spend his time doing the Lord's work and thinking how*

to please him. But a married man has to think about his earthly responsibilities and how to please his wife. His interests are divided. In the same way, a woman who is no longer married or has never been married can be devoted to the Lord and holy in body and in spirit. But a married woman has to think about her earthly responsibilities and how to please her husband. I am saying this for your benefit, not to place restrictions on you. I want you to do whatever will help you serve the Lord best, with as few distractions as possible. (1 Corinthians 7:32–35 NLT)

(To better understand this Scripture, you should read all of 1 Corinthians 7.)

Once Eve was created, Adam was distracted with the concerns of Eve. Of course, it was God's idea to create Eve because it was not good for Adam to be alone. Keep in mind that our knowledge of good and evil is to come from *all* God says. He also says, *"He who finds a wife finds a good thing, and obtains favor from the Lord"*[2] and *"Marriage is honorable among all, and the bed undefiled; but fornicators and adulterers God will judge."*[3] God created mankind not just for relationship with Himself, but also for relationship with others, especially a spouse.

It also appears that God did not immediately give Adam and Eve children. Was this so that God could have

[2] see Proverbs 18:22.
[3] see Hebrews 13:4.

more time with Eve? For if Eve would have had children right away, she would have been doubly distracted with Adam and a child. We do not know how long God had with Eve before she had children, but I do believe that God wanted special time with Eve just as with Adam.

The purpose of the Garden of Eden was to be a place of companionship. I see this purpose in three aspects—the first aspect being companionship with Adam, the second aspect being companionship with Adam *and* Eve, and the third aspect being companionship with their family.

Applying this purpose to our lives, I see God first desiring companionship with each of us individually (men, women, and children). Then second, for those who marry, He desires companionship with husbands and wives as a couple. Then third, for those who have children, He desires companionship with the whole family. Yes, God desires companionship with whole families:

> *So they said, "Believe on the Lord Jesus Christ, and you will be saved, you and your household." (Acts 16:31)*

The greatest fruit you can bear is your love relationship with God. This most important fruit in your life grows and matures just as fruit on a tree, which starts as a bud and ends as mature fruit (unless something stops its growth). The next most important fruit you can bear is your love relationship with others; it too grows as fruit on a tree does.

As Adam and Eve began to know God intimately, the devil attempted to disrupt their relationship. How? By attacking the love that God had for them. Specifically, he attacked the two basic parts of love, which are protection and provision. In effect, love *is* protection and provision. But in the Garden, Satan attacked God's love for Adam and Eve by saying that He was *not protecting* them from death, and that He was *not providing* for all their needs:

> *Then the serpent said to the woman, "You will not surely die. For God knows that in the day you eat of it your eyes will be opened, and you will be like God, knowing good and evil." (Genesis 3:4–5)*

Eve was deceived when she questioned God's love for her. We too are deceived anytime we question God's love for us. Of course, we have all been assaulted with this temptation to doubt God's love. Even so, I have found that the best way for me to overcome this temptation is to remember Jesus—His life, His sufferings, His death, and His resurrection.[4] By looking to Jesus, I see the absolute proof of God's love for me—He is my protection and my provision!

Placed in His Garden

So far in this book, I have stressed how we are His garden. Now I want to add to this truth by looking at the following verse again:

---

4 see Hebrews 12:2–3.

The Lord God planted a garden eastward in
Eden, and there He put the man whom He
had formed. (Genesis 2:8)

About 2000 years ago, God formed another "garden"
and He placed us in it—the body of Christ—the church.
Just as we individually are His "Garden of Eden," so
corporately we are His "Garden of Eden"[5] (the word
Eden means "pleasure").[6] Thus, individually and
corporately, we are *His garden of pleasure.* As God
made the first garden according to His good pleasure in
Eden, so He also formed this new "garden" (the body of
Christ) according to His pleasure:

But now God has set the members, each one
of them, in the body just as He pleased.
(1 Corinthians 12:18)

As God brought each pair of creatures into the
Garden of Eden, they added something special to it.
However, God *first* brought them to Adam so he could
identify them. Therefore, it is also important that we
help identify those added to the local body of Christ.
Who are they? What makes them special? What gifts do
they have that will add to the body of Christ? The
twelfth chapter of 1 Corinthians and several other
Scriptures will help us identify each person's giftings.
Then, let's allow God to place them where they will bear
the most fruit. At times, this means they may have to go
to another local church, or they may have to come from
another local church to "your church."

---

5 see 1 Corinthians 12:27.
6 Brown-Driver-Briggs Hebrew Lexicon—Abridged.

It is also interesting to note that God brought three kinds of creatures to Adam, the cattle (domestic-type animals), birds of the air, and the wild animals. In the same way, God places three kinds of *His new creations*[7] into His church:

> "Domesticated" new creations—those raised in church, or those somewhat moral.
> "Birds of the air" new creations—those who already soar spiritually.
> "Wild" new creations—those coming out of the world with little or no morals.

All three types of God's new creations are vital for the local church. However, many churches try to attract only one or two of these groups, but all are necessary for a healthy church. If you only want those who already have a soaring knowledge of God, then you are depriving yourself of a great blessing and a command of Jesus—to make disciples.[8]

We do not know how much Eve knew of God before she was brought to Adam. But it could be much more than commonly thought. Remember, God placed Adam in a deep sleep (possibly a coma-type sleep) before making Eve. I always assumed that Adam only slept while God *"took one of his ribs, and closed up the flesh in its place."*[9] However, we do not know how long Adam was in this deep sleep.

---

7 see 2 Corinthians 5:17.
8 see Matthew 28:19–20.
9 see Genesis 2:21.

The Bible says that after God made Eve, He *brought* her to Adam.[10] By God bringing her to Adam, it shows that she was not made alongside Adam; she was made somewhere else. Why would this be important? I think that God did it that way so that He could have time with Eve before bringing her to Adam—to build at least some relationship with Eve before bringing her to Adam. In doing this, God is showing us that He first wants personal relationships with women as well as with men.

It is important to know that Eve was first with God before being brought to Adam—to show that her relationship to God was first, then, her relationship with Adam. So however long it was before she was brought to Adam, that time was spent with God. She knew God *before* she knew Adam! Also, it is interesting to note that although Adam saw God first in the Garden of Eden, a woman saw the resurrected Christ first at the Garden Tomb.

As Adam and Eve had the privilege of teaching each other what they had learned about God and His creation before meeting each other, so it is with us today. We are to teach and to be taught about God and His creation—a major purpose of the church. Even so, the church should *especially* be teaching about the heart of God and His heart for His creation. We see from how God created the first humans that He is first concerned about relationships, which is the church's main job description—to develop strong loving relationships with God and others. Jesus said:

---

[10] see Genesis 2:22.

> *"By this all will know that you are My disciples, if you have love for one another."* *(John 13:35)*

Certainly, love is the greatest fruit we can bear; and God has given us a great place for our love to grow—the church. Keep in mind the initial command to be fruitful and multiply was given in the Garden of Eden—the initial place of fruitfulness (but Adam and Eve failed); however, the last Adam, Jesus, birthed another garden—the church (the second "Garden of Eden"), which has been fruitful and has multiplied. Without question, a major portion of our fruit is to be produced within this garden—the church.

Another place to bear much fruit is within the home. As parents, we teach our children to love God and to love others; then, as family members, we grow in love for each other, which facilitates great fruitfulness.

The main fruit and main purpose of the Garden of Eden was to know the heart of God. The main fruit and main purpose of your *Life in God's Garden* is to know God, to know His heart. To know His heart is to know true love.

The Bible speaks of knowing the width, length, depth, and height of God's love. I have always thought that we can each individually know the extent of His love. However, recently I have a deeper understanding of what the Bible says.

> *... And I pray that you, being rooted and established in love, may have power, together with all the saints, to grasp how*

wide and long and high and deep is the love
of Christ . . . (Ephesians 3:17–18 NIV)

There is a depth of His love that can only be comprehended "with all the saints." In other words, we can know much about the love of God ourselves, but to grasp His love fully, we must see His love for other saints (what He did for them and how they understand His love). This is something we will spend eternity doing—going to billions of saints and hearing of how God loved them. In doing this, with each person's revelation of God's love expressed to them, we will grasp a greater understanding of the width, length, depth, and height of God's love. For sure, this will be one of the greatest highlights of our heavenly experience. However, we are not to wait to get to heaven to do this. Even now, we can listen to other Christians and hear about God's love shown to them. Yet, God's love is not limited to the saints; He also loves those who do not know Him. This too gives us a new and better understanding of His great love—that He is not willing that any should perish, but that all should come to repentance.[11]

Fruit of the Spirit

The fruitfulness of the church is about to increase dramatically as it becomes the army of God that it is meant to be. With this change, the church will fully use its most powerful weapons resulting in abundant fruitfulness—bringing many people to Christ.

---

[11] see 2 Peter 3:9.

> *We are human, but we don't wage war as*
> *humans do. We use God's mighty weapons,*
> *not worldly weapons, to knock down the*
> *strongholds of human reasoning and to*
> *destroy false arguments. We destroy every*
> *proud obstacle that keeps people from*
> *knowing God. We capture their rebellious*
> *thoughts and teach them to obey Christ.*
> *(2 Corinthians 10:3–5 NLT)*

The church, as God's army, will do in the coming days what these verses say; and in so doing, they will be the army God has made them to be. The fruit of this army will be *"destroying every proud obstacle that keeps people from knowing God and capturing their rebellious thoughts and teaching them to obey Christ."*

The first visible fruit man produced was working with God to name His creation. God did the creating, but Adam did the naming. So it is with the church; God does the birthing by His Spirit and adds him or her to the church, then we do the *naming*, which is the commission Jesus gave to the church:

> *"All authority has been given to Me in*
> *heaven and on earth. Go therefore and make*
> *disciples of all the nations, baptizing them in*
> *the **name** of the Father and of the Son and of*
> *the Holy Spirit, teaching them to observe all*
> *things that I have commanded you . . ."*
> *(Matthew 28:18–20 emphasis added)*

We are to make disciples by immersing them into the *name* of the Father, Son, and Holy Spirit. This is more than just immersing them as a son or daughter of the Father, or as a brother or sister of the Son, or as a temple of the Holy Spirit. We are to make disciples by immersing them into the name (the character of) Father, Son, and Holy Spirit. To say it another way, we are to immerse them into the personality, the character, the qualities of the Father, of the Son, and of the Holy Spirit. We are to make disciples by submerging them into the nature of each of the persons of the Godhead because we all need a living relationship with each of the persons of the Godhead. As the Scriptures show, we can know each person of the Godhead in a special way:

> *May the grace of the Lord Jesus Christ, the love of God, and the fellowship of the Holy Spirit be with you all. (2 Corinthians 13:14 NLT)*

The *central* purpose of *Life in God's Garden* is to know God intimately as Father, Son, and Holy Spirit. There is nothing more fulfilling as His garden than to know the love of the Father, the grace of Jesus Christ, and the fellowship of the Holy Spirit. That is, to have *complete* fulfillment in your life you must have an intimate relationship with all three persons of the Godhead. To gain your *full* fruitfulness requires a relationship with all of the Godhead. Remember, you came to Christ because of the love of the Father,[12] and you know Christ through the Holy Spirit.[13] Because of this, you are able to bear fruit by the power of the Spirit.

---

[12] see John 3:16, 6:44 and 1 John 4:19.
[13] see John 14:26.

Why does a fruit tree bear fruit? Because it is a fruit tree. If it is planted in good soil and watered, it will produce fruit. The same is true of us; we will bear fruit if we stay rooted and grounded in Jesus Christ. We can only do this by the power of the Holy Spirit.

Another major purpose of *Life in God's Garden* is to learn to walk in the Spirit. I like the words *walk in the Spirit* because they break down the life in the Spirit into steps—one after another. Just as life in the Garden of Eden was about choices, so is your life in the garden of God today. Each choice is a step either to walk in the Spirit or to walk in the flesh. In light of this, what step will you take as the next choice is before you? Will you take a step in the Spirit or a step in the flesh?

Keep in mind that you are where you are today because of the choices you have made—the steps you have taken. Simply put, you are where you are in your relationship with God because of the steps you have taken. In fact, you are as close to Him as you have chosen to be.[14]

Furthermore, you are where you are in your prayer life because of your choices. Also, your marriage and family is where it is today because of your choices. Good choices (walking in the Spirit) bring life, but bad choices (walking in the flesh) bring corruption.

> *Don't be misled: No one makes a fool of God. What a person plants, he will harvest. The person who plants selfishness, ignoring the needs of others—ignoring God!—harvests a*

---

[14] see James 4:8.

crop of weeds. All he'll have to show for his life is weeds! But the one who plants in response to God, letting God's Spirit do the growth work in him, harvests a crop of real life, eternal life. (Galatians 6:7–8 TMSG)

The Bible enables us to bear the fruit of the Spirit by making our path to walk on very plain:

I say then: Walk in the Spirit, and you shall not fulfill the lust of the flesh. For the flesh lusts against the Spirit, and the Spirit against the flesh; and these are contrary to one another, so that you do not do the things that you wish. But if you are led by the Spirit, you are not under the law.

Now the works of the flesh are evident, which are: adultery, fornication, uncleanness, lewdness, idolatry, sorcery, hatred, contentions, jealousies, outbursts of wrath, selfish ambitions, dissensions, heresies, envy, murders, drunkenness, revelries, and the like; of which I tell you beforehand, just as I also told you in time past, that those who practice such things will not inherit the kingdom of God.

But the fruit of the Spirit is love, joy, peace, longsuffering, kindness, goodness, faithfulness, gentleness, self-control. Against such there is no law. And those who are Christ's have crucified the flesh with its passions and desires. If we live in the Spirit, let us also walk in the Spirit. Let us not become conceited, provoking one another, envying one another. (Galatians 5:16–26)

As a weak human being, making the right choice is not always easy; however, you and I have the grace of God available to help us whenever we need help.[15] By His grace, we can walk in the power of the Spirit.

Jesus always asks the right questions—ones that cause us to examine our hearts:

"A good tree can't produce bad fruit, and a bad tree can't produce good fruit. A tree is identified by its fruit. Figs never grow on thornbushes, nor grapes on bramble bushes. A good person produces good things from the treasury of a good heart, and an evil person produces evil things from the treasury of an evil heart. What you say flows from what is in your heart.

"So why do you keep calling me 'Lord, Lord!' when you don't do what I say?" (Luke 6:43–46 NLT)

Obedience to Christ is the fruit God is looking for, which is produced by *walking* in the Spirit. Yes, you are in Christ, but the fruit God is looking for is Christ *in you*—that Christ comes through you—you reveal His nature in your life. That part of Jesus' nature expressed through you is the fruit that you bear.

---

[15] see Hebrews 4:15–16.

Jesus is the great intercessor, healer, deliverer, apostle, prophet, evangelist, pastor, teacher, counselor, etc. And all of the manifestations of the nature of Jesus that come through you are to be coupled with the fruit of the Spirit. Specifically, you will intercede, heal, deliver, teach, pastor, evangelize, prophesy, etc. with love, joy, peace, longsuffering, kindness, goodness, faithfulness, gentleness and self-control.

The fruit of the Spirit is what is grown in God's garden today (you and the church). When the church uses its weapons coupled with the fruit of the Spirit, it will prevail through any darkness.

Let's close this chapter by looking at something that is beyond our understanding—how we as weak human beings can give God great glory:

> *"I am the true grapevine, and my Father is the gardener. He cuts off every branch of mine that doesn't produce fruit, and he prunes the branches that do bear fruit so they will produce even more. You have already been pruned and purified by the message I have given you. Remain in me, and I will remain in you. For a branch cannot produce fruit if it is severed from the vine, and you cannot be fruitful unless you remain in me.*

> *"Yes, I am the vine; you are the branches. Those who remain in me, and I in them, will produce much fruit. For apart from me you can do nothing. Anyone who does not*

remain in me is thrown away like a useless branch and withers. Such branches are gathered into a pile to be burned. But if you remain in me and my words remain in you, you may ask for anything you want, and it will be granted! **When you produce much fruit, you are my true disciples. This brings great glory to my Father.**

"I have loved you even as the Father has loved me. Remain in my love. When you obey my commandments, you remain in my love, just as I obey my Father's commandments and remain in his love." (John 15:1–10 NLT emphasis added)

This passage of Scripture shows how serious God is about us bearing fruit, for He cuts off those who do not bear fruit! And those who do bear fruit, He prunes so that they will bear more fruit.

Your greatest fruit producing potential is in abiding in Him—making your home in His love. When you obey his commandments, you abide in His love—the distinguishing characteristic of being His disciple. These disciples bear much fruit, which brings great glory to God. You can do it! YOU can bring great glory to God! Simply remain in His love.

Therefore by Him let us continually offer the sacrifice of praise to God, that is, the fruit of our lips, giving thanks to His name. But do not forget to do good and to share, for with such sacrifices God is well pleased. (Hebrews 13:15–16)

As God's garden, we are to be fruitful and multiply. For this reason, our garden will be inviting to others; our garden (our life) will cry out to them as they pass by it. By being God's garden, it will stir within others a deep desire for their own garden-type life. Then we may invite them to experience the life that is in Jesus Christ.

"Is anyone thirsty?
Come and drink—
even if you have no money!
Come, take your choice of wine or milk—
it's all free!
Why spend your money on food that does
not give you strength?
Why pay for food that does you no good?
Listen to me, and you will eat what is good.
You will enjoy the finest food.

"Come to me with your ears wide open.
Listen, and you will find life. . . ."

Seek the Lord while you can find him.
Call on him now while he is near.
Let the wicked change their ways
and banish the very thought of doing
wrong.
Let them turn to the Lord that he may have
mercy on them.
Yes, turn to our God, for he will forgive
generously. (Isaiah 55:1–7 NLT)

Just as the Bible began with God desiring humanity's fellowship, so it closes with the same:

> *And the Spirit and the bride say, "Come!" And let him who hears say, "Come!" And let him who thirsts come. Whoever desires, let him take the water of life freely. (Revelation 22:17)*

I will close this chapter with a quote from my pastor that summarizes how we bear fruit:

> *"He does the work; we do the walk."*
> —*Pastor Christie DeWees.*

My son, Austin, will take us on a wonder-filled journey into the Lord's enclosed garden in the next chapter.

Chapter 7

The Enclosed Garden

by Austin J. Campbell

Genesis 2:1 makes it clear that God created the heavens and the earth. In Colossians 1:16, we see whom everything was made through and for—Jesus. Indeed, He is the reason why everything exists; it is for His pleasure and for His purposes.

> *For everything, absolutely everything, above and below, visible and invisible, rank after rank after rank of angels—everything got started in him and finds its purpose in him. (Colossians 1:16 TMSG)*

Because everything is for Jesus, our eternal destiny must be wrapped up in how Jesus thinks and feels about us. The Bible also makes it clear that He has great love for the whole world,[1] as well as for His disciples;[2] so knowing the love that Jesus has for humanity is one of the most important truths about God. Without the knowledge of this love, He would be just like any other run-of-the-mill god out there. Even so, there is a distinction made for those who receive Him as Savior and Lord—He *enjoys* His people!

---

[1] see John 3:16.
[2] see John 15:9.

The Lord takes pleasure in those who fear
Him,
In those who hope in His mercy.
(Psalm 147:11)

How marvelous is this truth! God not only loves His people, He really enjoys the relationship. A great example of God's pleasure over His people is found in Song of Solomon chapter four, where king Solomon compares the love he has for his bride with a beautiful garden.

A garden enclosed
Is my sister, my spouse,
A spring shut up,
A fountain sealed.
(Song of Solomon 4:12)

I believe all Scripture points to Jesus,[3] so let's look at this verse through the lens of Jesus as our divine Bridegroom. Jesus' bride (the church) is compared to an enclosed garden, a place of pleasure and fulfillment, something harkening back to Eden. It would seem we are God's personal Garden of Eden.[4]

The garden described in the above verse was not one made out of necessity (one cultivated for the sole purpose of providing food), it was a special garden created exclusively for Solomon's pleasure. Although some fruit trees and more were in this garden, the selection of each plant in the garden was whatever the king desired. Thus, this place had the most beautiful and

---

[3] see Luke 24:27.
[4] see 1 Corinthians 3:6–9 and Isaiah 58:11.

fragrant plants around for giving rest to a king with many duties—a place where he could escape the stress of government and relax in his personal paradise. This garden was something he took pride in.

Much in the same way, God has created His own enclosed garden in the hearts, minds, and emotions of humanity. He made them to be irresistible to Himself. Obviously, He could have made us any way He wanted; therefore our design is exactly what He desired. We are desirable by virtue of being made in His very image, His very likeness. We are like an empty vessel that Jesus imparts His nature into.

I encourage you to take a verse like Song of Solomon 4:12 and pray it to God because there is great power in speaking the Scripture back to Him. When I pray, I say something like this, "Thank You Jesus, that I am your dwelling place and You take great delight in me! You call me Your beloved one. Jesus, I pray You would be my first love, and that I would remember I was made for You first, before anyone else. In trial and in blessing, may the fragrance of my obedience be pleasing to You."

When you put the Word of God in your dialogue with Him, the Bible becomes a part of you. I have found this to be the most effective way to learn the Bible. For if I pray the Scripture instead of simply memorizing it, more than just knowledge of the Word is gained, a passion for it is gained.

Three Enclosures

Humanity resembles an enclosed garden in three major ways:

The first way is the design of the mind and heart. Behind a veil of flesh is an invisible world more real than the one outside. Every action, the most kind and most evil, finds its origin there. The mysterious bond between mother and child comes from that secret place. The sacrifice a father makes to provide and protect is created there. Even the world we see around us would never be if not for the soil of the mind and the heart.

God created your inner self like a secret world, where it is God and you alone. It is in this invisible world where ideas and decisions are made. Enclosed in secrecy, where no one else can see, is a constant conversation going on inside the mind. Think about it: There is never a time when you're not thinking. This is how you can pray always, by inviting Jesus into the constant conversation of your thought life since prayer is communion with God, like what Adam had in the Garden.

Our design is fascinating! We have so many abilities as beautifully made creatures. We've climbed the tallest mountains, conquered the untamable seas, and even placed a man on the moon! Our ability to create has made all these impossible things possible, yet we've never been able to recreate the thing that makes us unique: the human mind.

There is another constant inside the mind, which is the imagination. As soon as someone tells us a story, our mind will be populated with pictures in our imagination. We have our own movie theatre that is open 24/7. The question is, what kind of films are playing there? I recommend inviting Jesus into this visual paradise by taking passages such as Revelation chapter four, where God shows Himself in the Scriptures, and fill your imagination with the beauty of God.

The final thing to point out about this invisible world is the emotions that reside there. These invisible feelings like love, joy, peace, anger, envy, lust, etc. are some of the most powerful things in our world, changing the course of our lives with just one moment of expression. How many people have had open doors of opportunity by one simple act of kindness? Conversely, how many stories have you heard of a family ripped apart by one act of lust such as adultery? For this reason, the writer of Hebrews warned against the dangers of immorality.[5]

As mentioned in the previous chapter, God is looking for the fruits of the Spirit, which are, *"Love, joy, peace, longsuffering, kindness, goodness, faithfulness, gentleness, self-control" (Galatians 5:22–23).*

When the three aforementioned motions of the soul (our thoughts, our imaginations, and our emotions) are touched by the Holy Spirit, then we can become loving, joyful, peaceful, etc.

The second way we are like an enclosed garden is the way God protects us. Since the reason for an enclosure is protection against onlookers or animals, and Satan is described as a roaring lion seeking to devour (1 Peter 5:8), God protects us.

> *But the Lord is faithful; he will strengthen you and guard you from the evil one.*
> *(2 Thessalonians 3:3 NLT)*

---

[5] see Hebrews 12:14–17.

God not only protects us from physical harm, but from spiritual defilement as well.[6] We can be sure there are countless things we don't even know about that we have been saved from by God's invisible hand.

> *My help comes from the Lord,*
> *who made heaven and earth!*
>
> *He will not let you stumble;*
> *the one who watches over you will*
> *not slumber.*
> *Indeed, he who watches over Israel*
> *never slumbers or sleeps.*
>
> *The Lord himself watches over you!*
> *The Lord stands beside you as your*
> *protective shade.*
> *The sun will not harm you by day,*
> *nor the moon at night.*
>
> *The Lord keeps you from all harm*
> *and watches over your life.*
> *The Lord keeps watch over you as you*
> *come and go, both now and forever.*
> *(Psalm 121:2–8 NLT)*

Third, the garden is enclosed by keeping the gate closed. Some translations use the phrase, "Locked up."

> *A locked up garden is my sister, my bride;*
> *A locked up spring,*
> *A sealed fountain.*
> *(Song of Solomon 4:12 WEB)*

---

[6] see 1 John 1:7.

The bride is locked up by virtue of keeping herself closed off to sin. She opens up to only One—Jesus. In Revelation chapter three, while speaking to the church of Laodicea, Jesus is seen as a gentleman, refusing to come through the door of the church without being invited in.

> *"Look! I stand at the door and knock. If you hear my voice and open the door, I will come in, and we will share a meal together as friends." (Revelation 3:20 NLT)*

Jesus desires our fellowship, to be with us, more than we can imagine. We are His great desire, so He is always near just waiting for us to respond to His beckoning. As mentioned in the previous chapter, you are as close to God as you have chosen to be.[7] His heart is always open and He is always ready to hear your prayers, so be confident in His kindness and give Him your time and energy.

God has designed you to be set apart for Him alone, and He protects the garden He has made, yet, just like in Eden, He gives you free will.

My Sister

Speaking about the position of the believer to His heart, He says, *"My sister, My bride."*[8] "My Sister" speaks of familiarity, one whom you are related to and know full well. In the Incarnation, God became man and dwelt among us.[9] He was no longer just our Creator, He

---

7 see James 4:8.

8 see Song of Solomon 4:12.

9 see John 1:14.

became our Brother, able to sympathize with our weaknesses.

> *We don't have a priest who is out of touch with our reality. He's been through weakness and testing, experienced it all—all but the sin. (Hebrews 4:15 TMSG)*

As your Brother, Jesus knows you deeper than any other person can, and He still chooses you. Even your deepest and darkest secrets are known to Him; and yet, He still pursues you. He knows who you are and He knows your potential. Even in your weakness, He says, "I choose you!"

My Bride

Being the bride speaks of the unique place in God's heart that a person occupies. It means nearness to Him like no one else can experience, not even the angels in heaven have this privilege. Out of everything God has made, only one type of creature is invited to be co-heirs with God in eternity,[10] and the only one chosen to be closer to His heart than all other created beings.

> *"And I have declared to them Your name, and will declare it, that the love with which You loved Me may be in them, and I in them." (John 17:26)*

As the above verse makes plain, God desires fellowship with mankind, and not just any kind of fellowship, but the kind that was already happening

---

[10] see Romans 8:16–17.

from eternity past between Father, Son and Holy Spirit—where God loved God in an unexplainable measure. Jesus' mission was to declare the Father's name (His essence, character, personality, etc.) and to continue to declare it for the next 2000 years via the Holy Spirit, so that weak and broken people could be transformed into His image and learn to love God the very way God loves God.[11] Our destiny is beyond anything we could imagine or think! To be able to love God and others in the same way the Father loves the Son is the ultimate happiness.

Our seemingly boring lives become exciting when we realize all of our prayers and studies of the Word of God have eternal significance. It is my prayer that the Holy Spirit has been declaring the Father's name through the pages of this book so that you can grow one step closer to the ultimate reality—the love of Christ being poured into your heart.[12]

The garden Jesus desires to live in is where there is only two—the thinker and the One whom you think about, alone in the paradise created for Him. Remember from Chapter 6 in this book: Adam was God's companion! He was created for God!

A Spring, a Fountain

At the end of Song of Solomon 4:12 there is mentioned a spring and a fountain, meaning the bride is a well-watered garden, as in, she is as healthy as she can

---

[11] see 2 Corinthians 3:18.
[12] see Romans 5:5.

be. This speaks of meditating on God's Word and listening to the Holy Spirit's voice, something reminiscent of Psalm 1:

> *Blessed is the man*
> *Who walks not in the counsel of the*
> *   ungodly . . .*
> *But his delight is in the law of the Lord,*
> *And in His law he meditates day and night.*
> *He shall be like a tree*
> *Planted by the rivers of water,*
> *That brings forth its fruit in its season,*
> *Whose leaf also shall not wither;*
> *And whatever he does shall prosper.*
> *   (Verses 1–3)*

The healthiest we can be on the inside is when we submit ourselves to the Holy Spirit and allow Him to lead us into all truth, for He will teach us who God truly is.[13]

The God Who Imparts His Beauty

The purpose of life is to know God; and by knowing Him in a deep and intimate way, we become like Him. To become like God was the promise the devil used to seduce Eve.

> *Then the serpent said to the woman, "You will not surely die. For God knows that in the day you eat of it your eyes will be opened, and you will **be like God**, knowing good and evil." (Genesis 3:4–5 emphasis added)*

---

[13] see John 16:13–15.

The devil knew the purpose of God's special creation, but he lied by claiming it can be attained through the "power of self"—by using the resources of the knowledge of good and evil to discern how to be like God. Apart from Jesus, our tree of life, it is impossible to be like God. Because of this, Jesus came and made known what the Father is like.

Surely Jesus will come again and all the nations will gather to Him,[14] and God's name will be fully declared, thus fulfilling the aforementioned promise of John 17:26. John made the same declaration again in his first letter:

> *Dear friends, we are already God's children, but he has not yet shown us what we will be like when Christ appears. But we do know that we will be like him, for we will see him as he really is. (1 John 3:2 NLT)*

The key to true happiness is the beauty of God, for He is a person of endless beauty. His personality, the way He thinks, and the way He feels is what makes life worth living. Certainly, the desire to gaze at and possess beauty resides in every heart, yet only the one who finds Beauty Himself will ever be satisfied.[15]

The fascinating thing about our existence is that God is not content to keep beauty all to Himself, He desires to impart it to us. Throughout the Song of Solomon, many times the woman is praised for having great beauty. Why is that? Obviously, people are beautiful to

---

[14] see Psalm 86:9.
[15] see Matthew 13:44.

God because they are fearfully and wonderfully made,[16] yet there seems to be another reason for the praise.

Could it be that there are two layers to our beauty, one by nature, another by the will? Think about it: The universe doesn't capture God's heart, yet it is breathtakingly glorious in its beauty. The high mountains, the great seas, the stars in the sky, and even the galaxies move His heart little to not at all. As we see in Psalm 33, God breathes stars into being, yet His focus is on the hearts of men.[17] Why is this? Could it be that the inanimate things of the universe were made beautiful by no choice of their own, no decision on whether to grow in beauty or not? However, as a matter of the will, humans have the unique ability to increase or decrease in beauty. By cooperating with the Holy Spirit, a person's personality can become beautified by submitting their desires to God. This is exactly what we see in Song of Solomon 4:9:

> *You have ravished my heart,*
> *My sister, my spouse;*
> *You have ravished my heart*
> *With one look of your eyes,*
> *With one link of your necklace.*

The small movements of your will fill Him with delight. You don't have to show Him love, but when you do, His heart moves with pleasure. Although imparted, your beauty is a chosen beauty. In the above verse, the reason for God giving the bride praise was for her effort

---

[16] see Psalm 139:14.

[17] see Psalm 33:6, 13–15.

to grow more beautiful. That is the fascinating thing about God—how generous He is when dealing with weak people. What is most marvelous is not that the bride is so beautiful (she is); it is how kind He is when searching her heart.

Unlike most people, who only appreciate art if it's perfect, God is like a tender father who hangs the sloppy drawings from his children on the refrigerator with pride—overlooking the crooked lines and out-of-proportion characters, for it is the sincerity with which it is given that makes it beautiful.

God delights in us even as we mature. The fruits of the Spirit may be in seed form or barely budding in our heart, yet, He still calls it beautiful. The Father has a big heart, and longs to show His tenderness. Listen to how He described Himself to Moses:

> *God passed in front of him and called out, "God, God, a God of mercy and grace, endlessly patient—so much love, so deeply true—loyal in love for a thousand generations, forgiving iniquity, rebellion, and sin. Still, he doesn't ignore sin. He holds sons and grandsons responsible for a father's sins to the third and even fourth generation." (Exodus 34:6–7 TMSG)*

From eternity past, God was this way; He has never changed, yet, until the creation of mankind, these aforementioned descriptions of God were unknown. These attributes of His character are only seen in how God relates to humans. He was not merciful to the devil, yet, He died for us. We are the canvas on which God displays His beauty.

Furthermore, it was God's idea from the beginning to impart His beauty to people. At the introduction of the Old Covenant, God instructed Moses to put His name on the children of Israel.

> And the Lord spoke to Moses, saying: "Speak to Aaron and his sons, saying, 'This is the way you shall bless the children of Israel. Say to them:
>
> "The Lord bless you and keep you;
> The Lord make His face shine upon you,
> And be gracious to you;
> The Lord lift up His countenance upon you,
> And give you peace.'"
>
> "So they shall put **My name** on the children of Israel, and I will bless them."
> (Numbers 6:22–27 emphasis added)

The purpose of the blessing was to put God's name on His people. He desired to impart His personality on Israel. Then, what do we see at the end of the story, when God is finally dwelling with mankind face-to-face?

> They shall see His face, and **His name** shall be on their foreheads. (Revelation 22:4 emphasis added)

The greatest destiny imaginable is for those who believe in Christ! The promise we have is that one day we will have the very name of God on our forehead, meaning His character and essence is imparted to us. Also, to have His name on the forehead means to be able to comprehend His nature. Even though eternity will be spent searching the depths of His personality, He will no longer be mysterious or hidden as He is now.

Knowing the depths of God's personality is the purpose of this garden called the human heart. Even though the fullness is not yet, it is still possible to have a glimpse of it now. We are designed in such a way that we are capable of beholding and comprehending, at least a little bit, who God is at any time we choose. Our thoughts, imagination, and emotions are constantly active, one just needs to fix their attention on God and find fulfillment and pleasure in Him, for He is our Garden of Eden. He is our resting place.

Conclusion

A dam and Eve experienced being in the Garden of Eden and then they experienced being driven from the Garden.[1] While they were in the Garden, they experienced rest; in contrast, they experienced sweat and toil, thorns and thistles outside of the Garden of Eden.[2]

In the preceding chapters, I wrote about many important lessons from life in the Garden of Eden, however, I skipped over two major verses until the conclusion of this book. In those verses, we see that God places a high value on His Sabbath rest:

> *And on the seventh day God ended His work which He had done, and He rested on the seventh day from all His work which He had done. Then God blessed the seventh day and sanctified it, because in it He rested from all His work which God had created and made. (Genesis 2:2–3)*

When Adam and Eve disobeyed, they lost their physical resting place (the Garden of Eden). Then, in Hebrews chapters three and four, we find that the Israelites did not enter into God's rest either. Also, in those same two chapters, we are given a serious warning

---

[1] see Genesis 3:24.
[2] see Genesis 3:17–19.

not to let it happen to us also. I will quote a few of those
verses here, but I recommend reading all of these two
chapters.

> *And to whom did He swear that they would
> not enter His rest, but to those who did not
> obey? So we see that they could not enter in
> because of unbelief. . . .*
>
> *For we who have believed do enter that
> rest . . .*
>
> *For he who has entered His rest has himself
> also ceased from his works as God did from
> His. Let us therefore be diligent to enter that
> rest, lest anyone fall according to the same
> example of disobedience. . . .*
>
> *For we do not have a High Priest who cannot
> sympathize with our weaknesses, but was in
> all points tempted as we are, yet without sin.
> Let us therefore come boldly to the throne of
> grace, that we may obtain mercy and find
> grace to help in time of need. (Hebrews
> 3:18–4:16)*

Grace is the power of God to live righteously, to
overcome the power of sin. When we believe His grace is
sufficient for us to overcome all our weaknesses, we
enter into His rest.[3] When we try to overcome sin in our
own power, we will not find rest because our rest is in
His finished work. His work of delivering us from the

---

3 see 2 Corinthians 12:9.

power of sin was finished on the cross. The cross is His grace, His power for our lives.

Most of the New Testament letters begin and end with the grace of Jesus, which is no accident, for the writers knew that the grace of God was vital for a victorious life. Therefore, in the beginning verses of most letters they start with *"Grace to you and peace from God the Father and our Lord Jesus Christ,"* or something similar. Then they close their letters with *"The grace of our Lord Jesus Christ be with you all,"* or something comparable.

Life in God's Garden requires the grace of God to keep it uncluttered—to be free from sin. Because of this, we simply believe God for His grace to live the life we were created for. In doing this, we can enter into His rest, His finished work.

YOU were created to be HIS GARDEN!

> *Now to Him who is able*
> *   to keep you from stumbling,*
> *And to present you faultless*
> *Before the presence of His*
> *   glory with exceeding joy,*
> *To God our Savior,*
> *Who alone is wise,*
> *Be glory and majesty,*
> *Dominion and power,*
> *Both now and forever.*
> *Amen.*
> *   (Jude 24–25)*

Join us on Facebook:

www.facebook.com/StevenJCampbellBooks

Author Steven J. Campbell may be contacted
at his personal email:
stevecamp3@hotmail.com

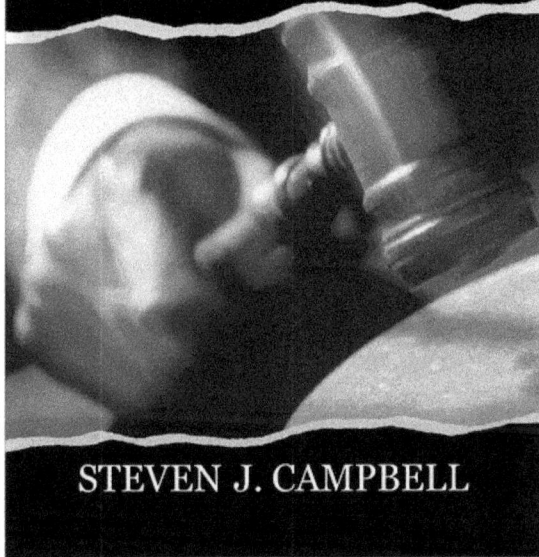

The Christian's Bill of Rights
A 31-Day Devotional to Help You Live Free

by Steven J. Campbell

This book is for helping you live in hope and the freedom Jesus purchased for you on the cross.

Well Done:
Good and Faithful Servant

by Steven J. Campbell

This book is for helping you to fulfill your purpose in the great end-time harvest and to hear Jesus say to you, "Well done."

Steven J. Campbell

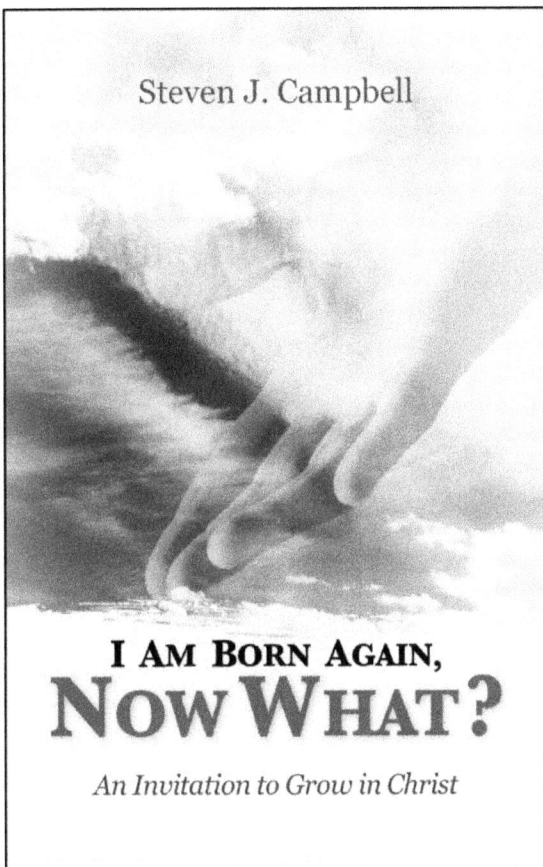

I AM BORN AGAIN, NOW WHAT?

An Invitation to Grow in Christ

I AM BORN AGAIN, NOW WHAT?
An Invitation to Grow in Christ

by Steven J. Campbell
and
Austin J. Campbell

This book is about growing in Christ in the basics of Christianity, experiencing His love in a greater measure.

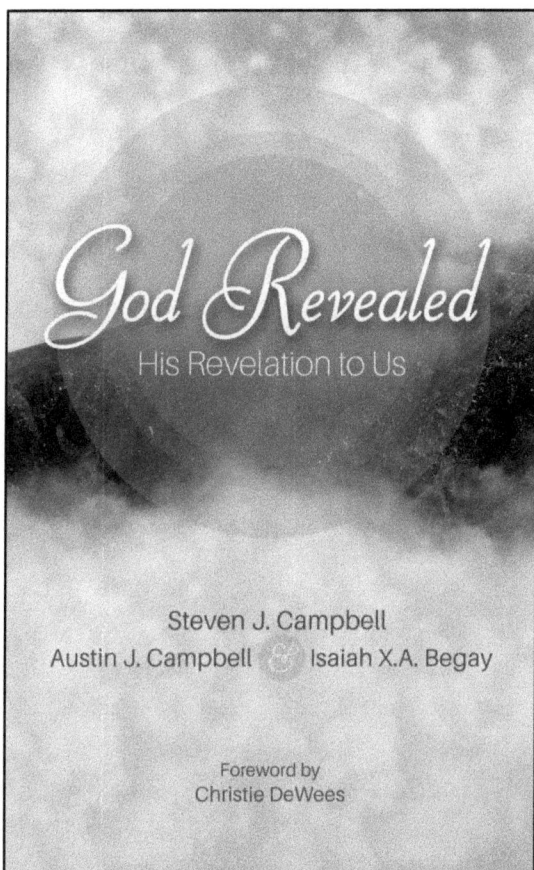

God Revealed:

His Revelation to Us

*by Steven J. Campbell
Austin J. Campbell
& Isaiah X.A. Begay*

The transcendent God—Father, Son, & Holy Spirit—decided it was time to be known . . . by creating mankind. This revelation can change your life.